A PRECIOUS BOND

How To Preserve The Grandparent-Grandchild Relationship

Susan Hoffman

Collegare Press

Collegare Press
P.O. Box 5622
Newport Beach, CA 92662

ISBN 13 978-0-9799168-1-6

Cover and interior design: Nita Gilson, Gilson Graphics
www.gilsongraphics.net

CONTENTS

Chapter 1
WHAT IT FEELS LIKE

Those of us living the nightmare of losing grandchild access all share a version of the heartache, frustration, helplessness and worry for the child's feelings. It has been said, that it's similar to that of a missing child, you know that they are out there, but you can't be with them. Taking a journey into the psyche of the disenfranchised grandparents may shed some light on the critical nature of preserving the bond.

A piece of our heart is missing, no matter how happy or fulfilled we become within ourselves, it can't be replaced.

Life goes on, as it should, and there are happy times in all of our lives. We feel joy doing fun things with friends and other family members; it's a treat to go out to dinner and laugh out loud at a funny movie, and to experience new places through travel, and to lead otherwise productive lives. But it's always lingering, that part of our self that remains empty. Even though we may get on with life, we never forget.

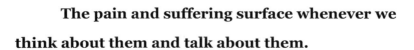

The pain and suffering surface whenever we think about them and talk about them.

Just when we think that the pain is subsiding, another emotional tidal wave hits us. We think that as time passes that we should be getting used to the status quo and therefore we should be toughening up. But, then something or someone triggers that 'thought' of the absent grandchild and the hurt comes bubbling to the surface.

Talking about feelings is healthy. It's better to get it out rather than holding things in, even if it hurts doing so. Experiencing the hurt and pain is an okay thing to do, and so is crying. What is hard is, never knowing when it's going to hit us. We can't always plan our "emotional time outs," so we have to accept that the triggers are out there and there's not much that we can do about it as long as the situation persists.

It feels like an open wound that is covered by a band-aid and whenever things start to unravel in our lives, the band-aid comes off and the wound festers once again. Whenever things go wrong in life, it's compounded by that constant ache and feeling of loss we have for the missing grandchild.

We all have those days, hours, minutes when things just fall apart. It feels like everything is going wrong at once and that is when the band-aid comes off. It is during our most vulnerable moments that the wounds become fresh again. The rent got raised, we got a pay cut, a friend stood us up, we lost our wallet and on and on, all part of life's ups and downs which have nothing to do with us missing our grandchild. Or does it? Because the wound will never heal, it's always raw and it is those down times that seem to exacerbate the hurt. I always notice that when I'm having a rough time of it, everything around me feels bleak, and most of all it strikes my weak spot, the part that will never build up immunity. My Achilles heel is that blank part of my soul where my relationship with my grandson should be.

We see a group of kids, and no matter where we are, even though we know it couldn't be them, we still look.

Am I the only one that does this? First I look even though I know it's not Jacob, and then I think to myself this is a little crazy, but that doesn't stop me. I continue to do it over and over, always turning around to take a second look, and being fully aware of my behavior the whole time. I can be anywhere, my own community or another city, whenever I see a dark haired boy from behind I always think and hope that it's him. Once I was in New York and told myself, " well, it could be him, maybe he's on a vacation?"

Our mind plays tricks on us when we want something so badly. We hope that we will run into our absent grandchild in the off chance that he or she is nearby through sheer coincidence. Maybe it's serendipity or maybe it's faith? If I wish it to be so, then it will happen. If I will it, concentrate hard enough, it will come true. This secret wishing game of expectation haunts us.

To be around other kids causes more pain than joy.

I thought that if I was around children that they would fill a void, not only for me but also the children, so I volunteered to work in a foster home. At first it was ok, playing cards and basketball; I bought drawing materials and taught some of the kids to draw. But then things got a little strange, I would show up for my shift and no one would be there. This happened more than once. I was getting the feeling that the home employees didn't appreciate having an outsider intrude. That particular home was a short-term facility so there were always new kids coming in to replace the ones who left, which made it hard to develop relationships, something that wasn't very good for my situation. When the politics became more important than the child's feelings, I terminated my position. Looking back, it probably wasn't the right fit for me. Although I still find myself thinking about some of the kids that I got to know there.

Generally speaking, I prefer not to be around children, I just can't do it. I suppose that I have completely shut off any desire of ever getting close to another child, it's easier that way. I just won't go there.

I can do this because I only have one grandchild, but for grandparents with more than one this is not an option. Everyone copes in different ways, and for some there may be some solace in being around other kids.

The only time that we get to be with them is in our dreams.

This is so true. It is while we are dreaming that we have the control. We are the director, producer and star of our own private movie. Sometimes the dreams are filled with so much joy because we have the freedom to be together, while others have an element of fear -- that of being caught together by the custodial caregiver. I have had those dreams myself, where Jacob and I are trying to find a way to be together and in the process we are sneaking and hiding from his mom. We are always on the run, dodging in and out of places, crawling under things, and seeking refuge. Once I had a surreal, extremely strange dream: In order to keep Jacob near me, I shrunk him and put him in my pocket.

There have been so many nights where I lie there and do everything in my power to will a dream, and try to program myself to dream of Jacob. I am not sure if that's possible, but I like to think that we have some power over our dreams now and again.

Seeing them from afar, in a photo, or on a social network is bittersweet. Even though it hurts, because they are out of reach, the alternative, waiting until they are eighteen seems incomprehensible.

We want to keep track of their growth. Photographs are essential, yet every time we look at them it tugs at our heartstrings. What's the alternative, to wait until they're grown to see what they look like? Maybe for some folks, me I'd rather have a small connection than none at all.

I am sometimes satisfied with a glimpse into Jacob's life, somehow it helps to feel like I am a connecting with him whenever I learn information or see a photograph.

Besides the small connection that I feel, I also like knowing that he is doing well. Grandparents are the overseers, they are the protectors of the child and just knowing that they are alright brings about some peace.

If you are so inclined to learn something about a grand-child and there is no other way to do so, I suggest doing some research, such as visiting a people finder website, obtaining an address, and then determining the school. Most schools have websites overflowing with information and many even belong to Facebook. If you want recent pictures, then either visit the school library and find the yearbook or call and ask who the school photographer is. Last, maybe volunteering in the school is an option. It's absolutely a gutsy move, but if it's a public school you have every right. I am not promoting clandestine maneuvers, simply introducing a few concepts that others have determined to be helpful.

Social networking is huge, and most kids over eleven are on Facebook, as are many middle schools and high schools; it is a public site so there is nothing illegal about checking it out.

As for obtaining a school picture from a photography studio, why not? You are the grandparent, simply call in the order, give them a credit card and have them mail them to you. This may be your only way to see the child grow up, and it's better than noth-ing, at least you get to see each year of their life.

We feel embarrassed, humiliated, and don't want our friends to know.

It's just simpler to put on our game face and pretend everything is fine.

We feel embarrassed that others will learn that our own children have treated us with such disrespect. We all want to be proud of our offspring. And when they fall short, somehow we believe that it is a reflection on us.

We feel some guilt about our own parenting as the cause for the breakdown. Did we do something wrong?

As a parent we also want to protect our adult child from criticism from others; it's ok for us to say something, but not outsiders. It's just the way it is, 'no one talks bad about my kid, but me" is an unspoken rule. So, the humiliation is about self protection and protection for our adult child's reputation.

It is just somehow easier to put on a front to protect ourselves and our child from public scrutiny.

I am not saying this is wrong because I don't think everyone has to know everything. There are some circumstances, however, when bringing the issue out in the open may help someone else.

Time and again when I'm talking about Advocates For Grandparent-Grandchild Connection, the person I am speaking with knows of grandparents in this situation. This always amazes me to learn that grandparent visitation issues are not that uncommon among families. It truly does seem to be a growing problem.

With so many people being denied visitation, awareness must be raised, which means talking about it to some degree.

There is support out there for grandparents and families and the only way to find it is to reach out to someone. Friends and family do not understand unless they have gone through it. With any recovery, it's imperative to connect with others in the same boat.

We live in fear that our grandchild may not remember us or may not want us once we find them when they are eighteen.

No matter how much we look forward to the day when our grandchild will be old enough to make his/her own decisions, that awful "what if" feeling creeps in. And it could happen, after all the kids in many cases have been brainwashed, or to use my invented term, "GAS", (grandparent alienation syndrome).

This happened to Jean Castagno, a pioneer expert in the grandparent rights movement, who has since retired. She started GRACE (grandparent and children embrace) an organization designed to help disenfranchised grandparents. She also fought a landmark legal battle in Connecticut so she and her husband could gain visitation with their three grandkids. They lost because the family was intact. Once the kids turned 18, she and Jules waited, and waited. Eventually they came around it just took more time, something the Castagno's understood all too well.

When we are ticking off the years, waiting in anticipation of that glorious day when the children will come knocking on our door, it never enters our mind that it won't come true. But then we start to hear stories such as Jean's and the feeling of dread seeps in. Our thoughts and expectations see saw back and forth between an excellent outcome and a dreaded scenario. After all, to find out that our grandchildren have no desire to connect with us at 18 may be even worse than the years without them, because at least then we had hope of a light at the end of the tunnel that our situation is temporary. Because after-all if that reunion is never to be, well then it's simply unbearable.

We have concern for the child's feelings of abandonment, confusion and sadness.

The second most popular comment that I hear from grandparents (the first being "I thought that I was the only one") is ""what about the child?"

Grandparents understand that a child's feelings are important, but parents do not. The parent is so busy being angry that it becomes the focus rather than considering the child's emotional well being. They are caught up in their own world.

The children have feelings such as confusion and sadness; after all, they love their grandparent, and formed a bond, so why wouldn't it hurt when the person disappears? Children form attachments which must be sustained and nurtured, not broken and ripped apart. Children suffer a loss of affection when a significant adult such as a grandparent is taken from them. There are serious emotional scars, not visible to the eye, but grandparents know this which is the source of their concern.

Grandparents feel enormous frustration because they are helpless. How do you stop the hurt, when you don't know what the child has been told? Are they told grandma is bad, or that she died, or doesn't love us anymore, or grandma's crazy, too busy, moved away?

It eats away at us, the unknown. If only we could explain, if only we could just say good bye. This is cruel indeed to cut the ties so swiftly and hastily.

Some children even blame themselves, just as they often do during divorce. There really is no good reason to remove a loving adult from a child's life absent dangerous circumstances. Ever.

Chapter 2

THE WHYS

The first question everyone wants to know, including sometimes the grandparent in question, is "why"? Why are you having visitation issues or why were you cut off completely?

"I don't know" may be a cop out. I believe if we go back and think about what led up to the situation some answers may come to us.

Another part of the "why" is that in any conflict, as the saying goes, "it takes two." As hard as this is to hear, there is truth to that wisdom. Even though it appears there are two distinct roles, a victim and a blamer, they are in fact interchangeable. In other words, the grandparent feels like the victim while blaming the parent who alienates them from the grandchild, yet the parent feels like the victim and blames the grandparent for causing the trouble.

No one is completely blameless when it comes to conflict; we all contribute one way or another. Sometimes it is the grandparent who fans the flames, knowingly or not. For those who unconsciously engage in behavior that may be destructive to grandchild access, there is information available in this chapter to correct the behavior.

Grandparents must become aware of what it is they are doing to contribute to the problem. By becoming conscious of potential trigger behaviors, grandparents can begin to right some of the wrongs.

Just to be clear, there is no superior judgment about right and wrong grandparent behavior or a set code of rules, instead it is what the parent considers right and wrong. That is the 'code of conduct' a grandparent must follow. Grandma Gail understood this well, and said of her daughter-in-law, "we call her the LAW." Gail knows all too well that to deviate from her daughter-in-law's code of conduct is to lose what she has.

This is true; the parents are in charge -- period, and they do not have to give a reason for any of their decisions. As erratic and unfair as their whys may seem, there is not much a grandparent can do about it unless there is substantial evidence of unfitness, abuse or neglect. Speaking up to protect a child is a duty of any concerned adult if a dangerous situation is sensed. There is a difference between true signs of abuse and a dislike for parental rules. Before taking action it may be in the grandparent's best interest to take a good look at some possible behaviors of theirs that may be causing tension or preventing access, and work on changing them. The goal is to build a cooperative relationship with the parents so that the grandkids remain in the picture. It is always better to head off the disaster instead of picking up the pieces and putting them back together afterward. Here are a few of the "whys" contributing to conflict between parent and grandparent.

CRITICISM

Grandparents are often quick to point out mistakes that they observe from the mom or dad. The parent may be doing something that you disagree with that may or may not have anything to do with the child, yet you say something about it. I had a client who made a derogatory remark to her son about the daughter-in-law's tattoos and of course he told his wife. Consequently she became angry and told grandma to stay away. Could this have been prevented? Yes, if the mother-in-law had kept her opinions to herself. All it takes is one seemingly small criticism to set someone off and put yourself forever on their do not contact list.

The golden rule applies here: If you can't say something nice....

Please keep your negative words to yourself or they may come back to haunt you as one of the reasons you cannot visit.

ADVICE

We are older and wiser, and made the mistakes that the new parents are about to make, so of course we want to save them from failure, especially when it comes to the welfare of our little grandchild. But slow down, this will surely backfire. Even if they ask for your advice, don't do it. They will resent it if you are right instead of being grateful and will blame you if you are wrong. This is too much unnecessary responsibility.

There are ways to politely work around this. Try first putting the request for advice back on their shoulders, by saying for example, "I'm not sure, what do you think". Or tell them, " you are better than I at figuring these things out".

If a parent presses for answers, offering up a few choices is another way to respond. If they perceive you as their equal and not their superior it levels the playing field and instills cooperation. By always being the recipient of advice, the parent loses self-esteem and the all-knowing grandparent becomes a bit of threat. Eventually the parent may see the relationship as a competitive one rather than a reciprocal one.

The following is an example of how to answer a solicitation of advice from a parent to grandparent. When the daughter-in-law asked the grandma about breast feeding versus bottle, even though grandma had strong opinions in favor of breast-feeding, she bit her tongue and responded: "thanks for asking, but it's such an individual decision, what does your gut tell you to do?" Grandma wisely kept her opinion to herself and shifted the responsibility back to the mom's shoulders.

CONTROL

Controlling the situation, any situation, can seem so subtle and harmless that we don't realize we're doing it.

Grandma Jan had been having some trouble communicating with her son-in-law and he suggested they have a talk during her next visit. Therefore, she was highly anxious about attending her granddaughter's next soccer game where the parents would also be. In anticipation of the upcoming talk, she thought it would be a good idea if she suggested that they all go for a walk following the game. Jan, by merely re-arranging the events, was trying to control the situation and didn't even realize it. First of all, the talk wasn't her idea, it was her son-in-law's, yet she wanted to take charge, yikes. No wonder they were butting heads. As it turns out, Jan enjoyed watching the game and seeing the kids and the dreaded talk never came about.

This instance was a perhaps a test of wills to see if grandma could behave herself and simply be a guest. Grandma was a career professional in business and was used to running the show, but this was not appropriate behavior outside of work.

In lieu of control, grandparents may well want to go with the flow. Controlling the environment at every opportunity does not make for a peaceful atmosphere. People who are controlling in nature tend to over-function in every circumstance, which can create resentment from the parents who desire to be independent adults. Time to rein it in.

TRIANGULATION

Grandparents who are having visitation issues are prone to solicit involvement from other family members and sometimes close friends with the hope of getting assistance. They think appealing to the son-in-law's parents will be a way to talk some sense into him. Many grandparents seek help from their other children to put in a good word for them to the parents of the grandchild. Procuring the intervention of a middleman is a way for the grandparent to avoid confronting those responsible directly. They are scared, nervous, and anxious that they may mess things up even more. They lack the necessary communication skills required to discuss matters effectively. So they defer to third party assistance.

When it was suggested during one of our support group meetings that a grandma may want to think about writing a heartfelt letter to her son, she responded that his sister was going to speak to him about the way he was treating her. This grandma was on good terms with her daughter and was willing to dump the responsibility on her to have a heart to heart with her brother, hoping he would see the light. The daughter had plans to visit her brother and his family and out of concern for her mother's grief over the loss of two of her grandchildren decided to come to the rescue. Grandma went along with it, appreciating all the support she could get. This way grandma could avoid a confrontation by letting someone else intervene and smooth out the problem. Well meaning family members or even close friends usually only make matters worse.

Involving a third party is not a wise move. The issue is between two parties, not three. The parents will resent the fact that the grandparent has sought help from outside sources and will feel like they are going behind their back, ganging up on them. The parents often feel that if you have something to say to me, say it to my face. It just rubs people the wrong way, and makes the grandparent look bad. It weakens their position, and takes away power. Please do not send family members to interfere.

Some grandparents think that by going to the other set of grandparents they will be able to facilitate the situation. This couldn't be farther from the truth. Grandparents do not necessarily stick together when it comes to this situation, fearing that they could be cut off themselves. They have too much to risk.

BOUNDARIES

Parents have their own way of doing things. They choose how they want to run their household and live their lives. They are responsible for raising their children the way that see fit whether or not anyone else approves. The exception obviously is abuse or neglect. Some parents are strict while others have a more loose approach to childrearing; either way it's their decision.

An example of a parental boundary is expecting grandma and grandpa to call before dropping by. That doesn't seem like too much to ask but for some grandparents it is.

One grandma worked right around the corner from her grandchildren's home and got in the habit of popping by on her way home from work. She would bring baked goods and little gifts, never arriving empty handed and of course never staying long; she just needed her quick grandbaby fix five days a week. Was that too much to ask? Apparently it was. Her son tried to speak to her about her uninvited visits and she brushed it off because she was simply dropping something off on her way home, thus it didn't fall under the "visitation" category. She thought that the tokens gave her a free pass. Daughter-in-law thought otherwise. She finally got so fed up with grandma's disruptions of their routine that she blew her stack. Grandma and grandpa were now banned completely from the house. The only time they saw the grandkids was if dad brought them over by himself.

Grandparents love spoiling grandkids with sweet treats

and presents, but once again parents most often want to be consulted first. Some grandparents have been known to pump the kid full of junk food and blame it on the kid, or have the child keep the secret. As for extravagant gifts, parents have been known to return them to the grandparent, which ends up causing hurt feelings and an eventual rift.

Grandparents must respect parental boundaries, no matter how silly they may seem, or face the consequences when they overstep them. Sometimes the consequences can be severe, making grandparents feel like they are being punished. They are.

I'M RIGHT YOU'RE WRONG

People in general seem to need to be right. It's human nature to want ourselves to be understood; it's good to have the right answer and it never feels good to be wrong. As a grandparent trying to establish a peaceful relationship with the parents of a grandchild, perhaps letting that need go would prevent future disagreements. One grandma said this about her daughter-in-law: "When someone pushes, I push back, I don't care who it is." Those words came to haunt her since she was constantly fighting with her daughter-in-law instead of letting things go. She has now been cut off as a result.

The grandmother let that urge to fight back get the better of her, and the mom and later the granddaughter, perhaps influenced by mom's attitude, became insolent toward the grandmother. Certain folks are fighters and won't let things lie. They are the ones who have the hardest time adapting to familial issues and working on them without a blow up. The ego takes over.

Contributing to the family feud with confrontations and constantly returning the serve will not keep a grandparent connected to the grandchild and the family. The desire to get things off one's chest because they have been gunny sacked (stored up and percolating) only creates a further "you *or* me" environment instead of a "you *and* me" existence.

Another granddad had to have the final word by sharing some wisdom with the parents. It's not that he wanted to fight; he just wanted to teach them a better way of doing things. This grandfather could not understand why their daughter wanted to be controlled by her husband to the point of complete isolation from all family members. It seems the son-in-law had moved the family, including, of course, the two grandchildren from California to Colorado without explanation. The grandfather shared that the father had reluctantly accepted money from him in the past and then had become accustomed to the assistance. When grandpa finally cut them off financially, the son-in-law was taken aback. No one knows for sure if the move was for financial reasons or to distance themselves from the domineering grandparent. The grandparents were heartbroken with the far away move and the alienation that followed.

The grandfather's solution was to educate the son–in-law about what was wrong with him, so he composed a five-page letter detailing his son-in-law's psychological problems and the remedies that should be followed. He was basically psychoanalyzing him and with treatment solutions. Grandpa, still clueless, couldn't understand why the son-in-law returned the letter with a note: "I can't understand any of this." Can you blame him?

The grandfather was on a mission to prove his son-in-law wrong and to blame him for the lost access but his approach was arrogant and self- serving. He honestly thought that sharing his wisdom and heightened sense of enlightenment that things would change and be different.

To shove your beliefs down someone's throat like that is surely sabotaging any chance of reconciliation. Psychobabble is best left in the therapist's office; nothing is more of a turn off than a neophyte practicing without a license.

Don't one up a parent, or try to prove how smart you are; you don't need to have the last word and always be right. There is a saying that wise people live by: "Do you want to be right or do you want to happy?"

GUILT

"After all I've done for you". It doesn't work. Reminding the parent(s) how much you have contributed to their welfare will surely sabotage the relationship. First of all they already know, and second there is no gratitude. Ever.

If grandparents harp on all of the good things that they do for the parents and grandkids, it will only make the parents angry and resentful, not a good idea. Lay off the guilt trip.

Giving should come forth with NO expectations. If a grandparent is not willing to give graciously then it's best not to give at all.

One grandmother continued to give money to the household fund and it was never enough because the parents just kept upping the ante. Whenever she didn't get what she wanted in the way of visitation, Grandma reminded the parents about her contribution and it only drove the wedge deeper and decreased the visits.

There are even grandparents who drudge up history about their parenting attributes. They tick off the list of all the good things they have done for their child while raising them and can't understand why they are ungrateful. Again. Entitlement. Please don't go there.

Chapter 3

YES, BUT:

Before the work begins a foundation must be laid.

In order for behavioral changes to occur there must be a willing participant. There must be cooperation rather than resistance or it won't work. Grandparents must be ready, willing and able to change any behavior that is a roadblock to grandchild access.

Grandparents who want to reconnect must be willing to do the work or else the plan won't be successful. They can be given the tools but unless they follow through, this guidance is worthless. One sign that grandparents are not ready to do the needed work is the "yes but" dialogue. Everything that is asked of them is met with a reason not to do it. Excuses.

Many people aren't willing to take a look at themselves and the things they are doing that causes the results they don't want. It's been established that we all get some sort of payoff for our behavior but that doesn't mean the results are what we want. We may feel empowered by standing up for ourselves and speaking our mind or we get a little fix for being right, but then we aren't allowed to see our grandkid as a result.

Letters and calls come in from grandparents across the country asking for support, education and solutions. The toughest part is the solutions, because it requires much work from the grandparent. They must dig deep within themselves and the psychological resources they possess.

Expecting another person to change behavior to suit our needs is unrealistic. The parents, most likely, are not going to change their behavior, yet so many grandparents hope they will. It is the grandparents who will have to change.

This is such a hard concept to grasp that many grandparents continue to reply, "yes but" when their actions are pointed out.

For example, when the parent starts reducing the visits by making excuses every time grandma calls, it's a red flag. This happened to Grandma Jennifer, who had once lived with her son, his wife and two kids until she found a job and was able to move out. She eventually did and moved close by so that she could stay near the kids she was used to seeing everyday. Shortly after, her son died in a car accident and six months later the surviving spouse got herself a boyfriend. The grandma kept her opinions to herself so that she wouldn't cause a rift with the daughter-in-law, which was smart. But grandma still expected to see the kids daily. It had been two weeks since she had seen them and she was coming unglued.

What Grandma Jennifer hadn't considered was that there had been a major change of circumstance with the death of a parent and that life as it had been would be different. She expected everything to continue as it had as far as her relationship with the grandkids was concerned.

Grandma Jennifer was calling the mother daily and when the mother's excuses became too much she confronted her by saying, "it sounds like you don't want me to see the kids." This put the mom on the defensive and of course she denied it.

I explained to Jennifer that calling every day was too much, things have changed, and she replied, "yes but I am used to seeing them daily."

Well, she won't be seeing them at all if she continues to pester the mom with daily calls. A better plan is to stop calling for a week or so and then call, and apologize for accusing the mom of keeping her away and then offer to pick the kids up on a specific day.

Sometimes the "yes but" appears before the contact is made; in other words it's used as buffer to avoid moving forward. For instance, "I can't call. They have my number blocked, or they never answer my emails." Every suggestion is met with a reason why it won't work, which is a "yes but" response.

Obstacles that grandparents manufacture sabotage their chances of creating a successful plan to reunite with the family after alienation. Overcoming these obstacles while in the tentative stages of alienations may prevent future turmoil.

While the obstacles to gaining access are real, such as the changed phone numbers, and addresses it's the grandparent's attitude about them that prevents them from conquering them. If every time an obstacle was put in our path and we let it stop us from moving forward, we would stop growing and not accomplish much. Sometimes grandparents do that when a parent presents an obstacle to seeing a grandchild. They let it stop them in their tracks, and don't navigate ways around it. They stop using their resources and become frozen and begin using the "yes but" dialogue.

The "yes but" grand says, "I can't contact them, I don't know where they live." The family may have moved without leaving a forwarding address, however with all of the available Internet people finders these days it shouldn't take long to get some information about the new location.

Suppose your calls are never answered and never ever returned? ." And if it is suggested that they send a card through snail mail, the "yes but" grandparent predicts the future by saying," why keep trying, they obviously don't want to talk to me."

No matter what ideas are suggested, they find a way *not* to solve the problem. "Endless Possibilities" are not part of their repertoire.

Please take a look at what you are doing and saying to yourself that gets in the way of taking action by doing the work that it takes in order to get back into that child's life.

Chapter 4

CHANGING BEHAVIOR: Yours, Not Theirs

We cannot change another person's behavior; no matter how hard we try we can't do it. So if we want to see a different outcome to a situation, then it is up to us to change what we are doing.

An insane person repeats the same behavior over and over and wonders why the results are the same. At some point it may be a good idea to take a good look at our existing behavior and consider looking for alternatives. For example, if grandparents are getting turned down for weekly dinners with the kids, yet they continue to make the same request week after week, perhaps, changing the tactic would provide the desirable outcome. The grandparents can give up the idea of the dinners and opt for another way to see the kids.

We may find that we take each rejection personally and our feelings get hurt or we get angry and frustrated when we are only trying to be close to our grandchildren. After all, we just want share time with them and be a part of their lives.

It is so hard to comprehend any kind of denial from the parents when our intentions are honorable; it just doesn't make sense. But we are probably the only ones who see it that way. The parents are not necessarily trying to cause hurt. Denied or reduced visits could have many explanations, some about the grandparent and some having nothing to do with them. Parents are busy, just as we were when we were raising our kids and sometimes it's hard to squeeze everything and everybody into the mix. Maybe that is all that it is, and if so, grandparents may want to figure a way to make the parent's life easier such as blending into their schedule instead of adding to it.

Don't expect the parents to change their behavior, to stop what they are doing in order to accommodate the grandparent's request. It doesn't work that way. The parents may not want to reschedule their routine so that the grandparents can see the kids on their terms. While it's great to have grandparents who want to treat the kids to a dinner out once a week, it's not always convenient for the family routine. Perhaps the parents consider it a disruption and don't want to deal with another variable. Maybe the grandparents', expectations of a rigid weekly schedule is off-putting to the parents. Whatever the reason, don't expect that the parents will change their way of doing things. The only way to get what you want is to change the way you are doing things, which means changing *your* behavior.

Let's use the example of the grandparents desiring a weekly dinner date. Perhaps they could reduce the number to every other week or whatever the parents are comfortable with.

The grandparents could also make the events less structured and more spontaneous. I understand that they want to see the kids on a regularly established basis, but something is better than nothing. Maybe dinner on a scheduled basis isn't working at all; there are other options such as showing up at sporting activities, or watching a dance class or piano lesson. Schools even have provisions for parents and grandparents to join kids for lunch. I think the grandparent needs to get creative and figure out other ways to stay involved without interfering in the family's schedule.

Grandparents may want to open themselves up to being the ones to change their behavior in order to remain a vital part of their grandchildren's lives. Set the ego aside, let go of any stubbornness holding you back from moving into new territory. Parents are not going to change, but grandparents are. It's the only way to avoid the threat of visitation issues or lost access. With the impending threat of complete denial looming, a grandmother couldn't see that she was the one pushing her son away. She had a history of quizzing her grown son about his personal life, specifically dating. "Do you have a girlfriend?" " I would like to meet her." She made demands was judge-mental, accusatory and played the "after all I've done for you", card. No wonder he was avoiding her.

In this case, fortunately her son flat out told her that the ball was in her court to change those behaviors in order to save the relationship.

Parents must perceive grandparents as non- threatening individuals. Of course grandparents never think of themselves as threatening, but others might. This is the reason the parent keeps the grandparent away just as they would anyone else they perceive as threatening. "You gotta make them want you around."

Grandparents must strive for an attitude change toward, "you and me instead of you or me" when it comes to getting along with parents.

If you want things to be different, if you want to get what you want, if you want to see change, then you are the one who will have to be doing the changing.

If you are willing to make changes, then you are ready for the next chapter.

Chapter 5
KISS BUTT

KISSING BUTT is a universal phrase which gets the point across. You can attract more flies with honey than vinegar. Be nice, even if someone is being a jerk, and you'll get more cooperation than when you respond from ego.

Why not apply this wisdom to our family? What could be a more important reason than our grandchild?

There are lots of words for it: "KISS BUTT, EAT CROW, EAT DIRT, KISS ASS," and my favorite, a Dr. Lauraism: "GIVE THE DRAGON WHAT IT NEEDS TO EAT." Be humble with the parent(s) because this will help you get along well with them and increases your chances of seeing the grandchild. The same goes for reconciliation; a grandparent may need to do some back-peddling to make things right by adopting a humble position – whatever it takes to get a foot back into a door that has been slammed shut.

Grandparents have often shared with me that it feels like they are always walking on eggshells. They probably are and may have to keep doing it. You can look at kissing butt in a derogatory way or you can tell yourself that you are just being smart about what it takes to keep the peace. Diffuse the situation rather than escalate it. Change your perception about what it is you are doing to stay connected and it won't seem so uncomfortable. When you make the choice to adapt your behavior so that it brings you the results that you desire, then it becomes more about accepting the reality of your situation rather than barely tolerating your position. You are in control because it's your choice. So what if you give the dragon what it needs to eat as long as it helps you to see your grandchild? Does it really matter how you got there? Use your intellect instead of your ego.

Often, parents need to feel they are right and they are the ones controlling the situation. Again, give them that. If you don't, there might be issues with grandchild visitation.

Getting Started:
I COMPLETELY UNDERSTAND

The first step in diffusing the situation is connecting. Acknowledge them. Some of the critical language that gets the point across to the parent is letting them know that you hear them and understand them. For example, "I completely understand your feelings." "I completely understand how you would think that." "I understand that you are upset."

Grandparents must come across as non-threatening; simply repeating to the parent what you hear them saying and acknowledging them will stop them in their tracks.

DON'T DEFEND, LISTEN INSTEAD

Do not defend your actions -- ever. When a parent is critical and confrontational, pointing out something that you did, the last thing they want to hear is why you did it. They want to be heard, not bulldozed over with your reasons for doing it. Just listen to them, nod, and then thank them for sharing their feelings. It's okay to say that you understand.

So, listen, say thank you, and I understand. You have nipped it in the bud. You have used your rational calm side to diffuse a battle and hopefully create time with a grandchild.

Grandparents Lana and Henry had not seen their granddaughter in three years because their son and daughter-in-law had cut them off without explanation. Lana continued to send cards and heartfelt letters, until one day she decided to simply ask what else could be done to reconnect. "Have I done everything that I could to make amends? If not please tell me what I can do."

That direct approach, perhaps combined with three years to cool off, prompted a response. The son replied with a scathing letter filled with criticisms of the parents, from nitpicky stuff like "you're rude to waiters" to "you don't communicate," or "you're always traveling." He ended the letter stating that although they would like to have grandparents in their daughter's life, they would have to prove themselves before any reunification was forthcoming.

Lana swallowed her pride and responded with not one defensive reply. Instead, the letter we drafted consisted of a thank you for responding. Remember it had been three years, so some appreciation was in order. The second part of her letter agreed with him by acknowledging his assessment, giving him the satisfaction of being heard. The third part explained to the son what they were doing to rectify the situation. Parents will see right through it if grandparents simply say that they are sorry and will never do it again. That's not good enough; they need proof that the grandparent has taken steps to truly make strides toward behavioral change. Tell the parent you understand what they are saying or that they are right. Once you have successfully completed therapy or the behavioral work, tell them you will contact them. Then what can they say? Not only is there remorse, but active measures have been taken to improve and rehabilitate the behavioral mistakes.

There is not an argument forthcoming if you agree with them. As in Lana's case, after she sucked it up, she told her son that she and his dad were working with a therapist as well as a grandparent support group, and they were making progress and would keep him in the loop about their readiness to be the kind of parents and grandparents that he expected.

Lana and Henry set their egos aside and focused on doing whatever it took to get their granddaughter back. After a few more letters and then a phone call, they met with their son alone and seemed to pass the test. A week later they got to see their granddaughter. Since it had been three years, the child had forgotten them so they met in a park. The parents re-introduced them for an unforgettable day, where they seemed to pick up from where they left off. Their little granddaughter was so accepting of them and thrilled to now have grandparents, just like so many of her friends. And there was never an awkward moment.

COMFORT ZONE: AVOID IT

Don't allow yourself to ever get so comfortable that you lose sight of the fact that there are no guarantees when it comes to the grandparent role within the family. Keep your radar up and don't ever slip back into old habits.

Grandparents Lana and Henry continue to be a big part of their granddaughter's life, seeing her now several times a week. But they do not forget that what they have is potentially fragile even though it currently seems solid.

All it takes is one slip up, such as a "just kidding" remark or jibe or any step over the boundary and they could be back in the same boat as they were before.

In other words proceed with caution. Think twice before

opening your mouth.

BACK BURNER

Grandparents should think twice before expressing their feelings about the stolen weeks, months, or years that the parents have taken from them, and more importantly, the child. This requires willpower. Some manage to compartmentalize and file it away for a later date, maybe when the child is eighteen. For others it's a struggle to bite their tongue. For Lana it was easier than it was for Henry. He was angry with his son for treating them badly and selfishly ignoring their own child's needs. Henry was even more disgusted with his son's accusations. Lana, however, prevailed on her husband's better judgment and they agreed to form a united front by putting those angry feelings on the back burner and focusing on moving forward instead. It worked.

Save the talk for when and if you have it, and if you do, make it about your feelings and not the whys. Tell them how it affected you. All you can really do anyway is be responsible for your own feelings. If you have the need to express yourself so that you feel better, then do so in a non-shaming, non-blaming way, even if you believe what they have done has no justification. Do not have this talk as long as there is a chance you may end up back where you were. If you decide to confront, wait until the child is old enough to make his or her own decisions.

NO SHARING FEELINGS

Grandparents think that expressing their feelings about lost visitation to the parents will somehow tug at their heartstrings and make them regret the hurt they have caused. Not true. The parents do not want to hear about the grandparent's feelings. Some have boldly told the grandparents that their feelings are just not a priority.

This is a sad realization, especially if it is your child you are dealing with, but if it's the daughter-in-law or son-in-law, then it makes more sense, the in-law doesn't have that shared history of upbringing to connect with.

Maybe grandparents feel better expressing how they feel to the parents, but it won't help. It's best to confide in a support group, therapist or a trusted friend or family member. In fact, sometimes it can make matters worse because the parent may prey on your vulnerability.

Do not spill your guts hoping to make them understand your feelings about your grandchild or even emphasizing the child's feelings. They are the parents and don't need to be reminded by the grandparent about how the visitation issue is affecting the child.

SAVE FACE

Make it easy for them. Parents, most likely, will not take the first step toward reconciliation. Why? Ego or pride. When the grandparents take the initiative and pave the way to mending fences then the parents save face. The grandparent has provided a safe and non-threatening environment for the parents to step into encouraging peacemaking. The parents can feel like they are in control even though it is the grandparent who has taken the high road.

Again, even though Lana's son may have forgiven her in his heart, he most likely would not have swallowed his pride and stepped forward to make amends. It requires a courageous person to take the first step.

CHARGING BULL: GET OUT OF THE WAY

When the bull charges, step aside. Do not fight back do not get in the way. It will only escalate, just as it would if it's a real bull.

When people demonstrate their anger, it's best not to try to reason with them. Instead, remove yourself from the situation. The best way to neutralize a situation is to become "neutral" in your behavior.

Once again, do you want to be right or do you want to be happy? Let them be right, or let them think that they are right. It doesn't matter what people think, so don't waste your energy fighting back to prove a point.

DON'T TAKE IT PERSONALLY

Part of changing your behavior is changing the way you think about things. This is not about you, it's about them. Tell yourself not to take personally what others say to and about you. This is a difficult concept. Sometimes it requires developing a tough outer shell. It also requires practice. A good idea is to post an index card on the fridge or mirror and repeat the sentence daily, "Don't take anything personally." Somehow we all need to beat it into our heads until we believe it. In Don Miguel Ruiz's book, "THE FOUR AGREEMENTS," a practical guide to personal freedom, the second agreement is "Don't Take Anything Personally." He says, "Even when a situation seems so personal, even if others insult you directly, it has nothing to do with you." He gives the example of a person being told, "Hey you look fat." He points out when people take things personally it is usually because they agree with whatever is said. So, if someone says "hey you look fat", not taking it personally, may sound like, "I disagree, but you're entitled to your opinion, or "if you say so." Don't give power to their words they do not carry any weight.

It truly makes life easier once we master this powerful code of conduct.

A grandparent shared that her former daughter-in-law wrote her a letter filled with criticisms about her. The grandmother was so upset that she simply wrote her off and never wrote back. Grandma said she was so hurt by the daughter-in-law's words that it was best to stay away from her. Grandma was giving the daughter-in-law way too much power. Was there some truth to the words? What was it about the criticisms that created such a strong reaction from the grandma? It has now been six months since she received the letter and she is still talking about it. She is still holding onto the emotions and those hurt, angry feelings. She needs to let it go or perhaps write a response and either mail or not mail. This way she can release those emotions that are holding her hostage.

PUT ON A HAPPY FACE

This means keep quiet and put on a happy face in front of the kids.

Do everything possible to separate your true feelings about the parent(s) from your grandchild. Grandparents have a responsibility to support the grandchild and keep negativity to themselves. You may tell yourself that the child has a right to know the truth, whatever it is, but it's not the grandparent who has the right to tell them. Keeping quiet is only part of the charade; watch your body language too. Kids are perceptive, they pick up on everything. Sometimes it's the unspoken that can get you into trouble.

Carol has court ordered visitation with her granddaughter and her own daughter goes out of her way to sabotage the visits. There is a degree of brainwashing going on in between visits, but Carol holds her tongue whenever Chelsea, her granddaughter, asks questions. Chelsea constantly asks why she can't come spend the night at grandma's house instead of the few short hours that were mandated by the court. Carol never places blame on the mom, she simply tells Chelsea that they're going to do something else instead as a diversion rather than say mom won't let you.

If a grandparent is lucky enough to be able to spend time with the grandchild not one precious moment should be spent denigrating the parents. Enjoy the child to the fullest, and keep those negative thoughts concealed for the sake of the child's well being. After all, children yearn to see all of the adults in their lives who love them get along in harmony.

CORRESPONDENCE: Stay Connected

If all communication has come to a halt, then written communication may be your best option. The written word has a more powerful impact, and besides it's one sided. You can say whatever you want without an argument or without being interrupted. You can time and compose your thoughts and present them more effectively.

Sending emails, cards, letters, texts, should not be an opportunity to preach or scold, but to connect in a positive and productive manner.

Don't offer advice, suggestions of counseling, or long tirades of defending oneself. These written notes should be brief and friendly.

If an apology is in order, don't ever say, "If I've done something to offend you, I'm sorry." That is not an apology and just makes people angrier than they are. How many times can you remember in relationships when the clueless boyfriend said the same thing? It doesn't work, and the so called apology is not an example of taking responsibility for your own behavior. If you are going to apologize, then take full responsibility by naming the crime and not doing it again. Admit that you made a mistake, and that you are taking measures to stop doing it.

If you have nothing to apologize for, then simply mail a note or card, such as "Thinking Of You." Tell the parent in one sentence that you miss them, and not just the grandkids. Depending on the situation, write whatever is appropriate. If a parent has cut you off suddenly and without provocation, in other words simply dropped out of the radar, then politely call them on it. Send an email or letter saying, "it seems like there is something going on, what can I do to rectify the situation?" Another direct and tactful approach is, "I would like to meet you for coffee, Monday or Tuesday at 10 Am, how do you feel about that?" Get them involved in the decision. Try sending a peace offering, like a coffee card.

If there is no response whatsoever for months, or the parents have flat out told you to stay away, then continue to send holiday and birthday cards to the entire family. Gifts are a personal decision, but if you send one, then sometimes it's best to send to everyone. Parents are sometimes jealous. They are competitive with their own children, not wanting the grandparents to love the child more than them. Parents also are insecure and afraid that their child may love the grandparent more than the parent. All of these insecurities contribute to a difficult to navigate twisted road and this can be exhausting for a grandparent.

At some point, when too much time has passed, it's time to ramp it up to the next level. Send an action note and ask, "Have I done everything possible to make amends?" Once you have tried everything, then it's not unreasonable to pin them down. That kind of direct sentence may be just too tempting to ignore.

There are no guarantees and it depends on many factors, such as time gone by, timing, persistence and breaking down barriers.

RESOURCES

We all have untapped resources. Sometimes it simply requires a nudge to get us on the right track. Again we can only change our own behavior and never someone else's. So, if we are not getting the results that we desire, then we may want to try doing things differently.

There is never just one way of doing things; there are endless or infinite possibilities to solving problems.

As for grandparents encountering problems with parents blocking visits with grandchildren, perhaps the motto that came from Dr. Laura serves as the most effective cue to watch yourself, 'give the dragon what it needs to eat."

Chapter 6

CLOG THE COURTS

Every state has grandparent visitation rights laws. Most states provide standing in a court of law for grandparents when the parents are living separately (divorced or unmarried) and when one of the parents is deceased. Only a few states (Alabama, Mississippi, Rhode Island) allow grandparents to petition for visitation when the family is intact, in other words married and (/or) living together. About half of the states allow for petitioning the courts for grandparent visitation after a stepparent adoption.

When you think about it, what does marital status actually have to do with the relationship between a grandparent and grandchild? Nothing.

Someday, perhaps for legislative purposes, parental marital status criteria will be exchanged for the simple phrase "unreasonably denied" and all statutes will be uniform on a national level. For now, there are at least laws in place for grandparents to be heard in a court of law in order to see a grandchild if all previous attempts have failed.

This is a growing social problem. If this were not an issue, then the laws would not be there. However, navigating the system can be confusing and decisions about whether it makes sense to turn to the courts can be emotionally wrenching.

The grandparent visitation rights laws are there for the purpose of protecting and preserving the relationship between grandparent and grandchild. The least adversarial approach to conflict resolution is to try to work out differences without litigation. However, that is not always possible. Sometimes the only way to remain in a grandchild's life is to go to court. Having a court order signed by a judge and filed with the clerk of the court is a legal binding contract that must be enforced. Grandparents can think of the order as an insurance policy to keep the visits consistent.

Sometimes grandparents are hesitant to file a petition. They are afraid of escalating the alienation. They know that it will make the parents even angrier than they already are, and may possibly stifle any chance of reconciliation.

Another hesitation is they think it will put the child further in the middle, and make things worse for the child. Some grandparents fear the unknown or think they are not emotionally strong enough to battle in court. There is also the financial burden that comes with hiring an attorney. The last reason may be lack of desire. Some grandparents are simply not willing to fight in court. The reasons vary for some it's as saying it's a family matter – it should be worked out within the family.

The question I always ask grandparents who are on the fence: "Is it in your grandchild's best interest to have you in their life?" If so, then you may want to think about fighting for them. This is not to discount any of the aforementioned obstacles, but instead find a workable solution to deal with each and every person involved in the situation, and at the same time remain focused on the bigger picture: the child.

FUELING THE ANGER

The first concern most grandparents have about going to court is further escalating the anger of the parent(s). Remember, no matter what you do, the angry parent will remain the angry parent. We have little control over another person's responses or reactions. It's similar to anyone standing up for themselves in a court of law; there will always be consequences. Should you worry about the respondent's feelings as your gauge in making decisions about the best interests of the child? Going to court is adversarial. Someone will almost always be angry. Carol and Gil were willing to take that chance in order to let their granddaughter know that she wasn't disposable. Her words, "We couldn't move on without doing what we could. The pain and feeling of rejection we didn't want our grandchild to suffer was the driving force in our efforts."

When children and grandparents have a bonded relationship and a parent breaks up the physical part of the relationship by unreasonably denying visitation to the grandparent, should anger be a factor? Carol's daughter allowed her child to cry for her grandparents all the while having the power to stop her daughter's emotional pain, but instead expected her to just deal with it. Perhaps concern over angering the perpetrator is misplaced.

RECONCILIATION

As for reconciliation, this is always a possibility; however, how long do you want to wait? And yes, going to court does often diminish the chances of mending fences, but not always. It is a risk you are willing or not willing to take. If the grandparents lose, then they will really be out of the picture. Some parents have patterns of blowing up and getting over it, so if the grandparents are used to that kind of rollercoaster ride and are willing to wait it out, then perhaps court isn't the answer.

There is a saying that always helps me put things into perspective: "When someone shows you who they are believe them."

Wishing and hoping and waiting are destructive, not only for the grandparent, but also for the child. Diana, a grandparent client, had a strong case; her daughter and grandson had lived with her for seven years. The daughter was a single mom and depended on her mom, Grandma Diana, to help raise her son,

Diana's grandchild. One day, the daughter decided to move out of Diana's house and move into the new boyfriend's place.

When Diana made it known that she wasn't fond of the boyfriend, everything changed. Diana suddenly went from seeing her grandson daily to seeing him maybe twice a year. She considered petitioning the court for visitation, but was afraid that her daughter would get angry, and that any chance of reconciliation would be lost forever, and besides, she told herself, there was always the possibility that her daughter and the boyfriend would breakup and then she would come running back. It has now been five years with the daughter throwing her crumbs here and there in the form of short controlled visits, yet Diana tolerates it. Diana was paralyzed between fear of further alienating her daughter and wishful thinking that things would magically get better.

CHILD IN THE MIDDLE

Another reason grandparents don't go to court is out of concern for the child's position within the conflicted family dynamic. They don't want to further put the child in the middle of the adult discourse. This is understandable; no one wants to harm the child, but what about all of the children who are living in the middle of their parents' divorce? Our divorce rate would surely go down if more parents considered the child's position and the effects on them when parents are in opposition. The same goes with grandparents.

Adult conflict affects all family members, which is all the more reason to take measures to protect the child during the storm. It can be done, but sadly children often are used as weapons between adults.

It is, therefore the grandparent's responsibility to be the voice of reason and go above and beyond to help protect the child's feelings. A child's love for a parent and a grandparent should not be a contest; they should never have to choose sides.

THE UNKNOWN

Grandparents often have no experience in engaging the judicial system. The forms, the procedures, the vocabulary, facing a judge, the consumption of time, the delays, are all part of a world unfamiliar to most.

Stepping into new places that will impact our lives is scary. Anticipating a change of any kind can be fearful. With so much at stake the fear is compounded. What if we lose? A better question may be: What are you and your grandchild missing out on by being unreasonably denied visitation?

EMOTIONAL STRAIN

The emotional strain of a grandparent grieving over the loss of seeing a grandchild, and the added burden of court, may be more than a person can endure. Grief and mourning a loss, any kind of loss, can overwhelm our daily lives and keep us from accomplishing simple things. Our concentration and focus may be clouded by the sadness and the stress the separation brings. Taking on a legal case is a job in and of itself. We need to be at the top of our game because we are still responsible with or without an attorney. It's ultimately up to us to make sure that the job is done correctly. If an attorney is representing us that doesn't mean a free pass to relax. There will be documents to gather, information to be shared, dates to remember and paper-work to be scrutinized. People make mistakes, even attorneys and paralegals. We must pay close attention; we are our own best advocate. The same is true if we are representing ourselves, even more so. Do not rely on the self -help centers of the court to provide all of the answers, question everything and check and re-check before the petition is filed. A clear head is necessary, so make sure that the time is right and that you are strong enough in every way to go forward.

FINANCIAL BURDEN

I won't deny filing a lawsuit with an attorney is expensive. Most attorneys' hourly rate begins at $250, and adding in re-tainer fees, just to get started may put you out $1500. A retainer fee is money required by an attorney in order to begin a case. It's kind of like an insurance policy that they will get paid. Sometimes when the money runs out, it must be replenished and if not, then the attorney may stop working, which means if the case goes to court, you could be hung out to dry. Although some attorneys are willing to keep working even if the client is behind in payments, hoping they can recoup the fee later.

There are alternatives to using an attorney, which is called PRO-PER, when a person represents themselves. Most Superior Courts have a self-help center, with access to forms both online and in the building.

There are paralegals, who can be hired to fill out the paperwork, but they may not represent you in court. There are also public law centers, and legal aide services for lower income individuals, however, these places have a backlog and getting assistance can take a long time.

In Sacramento, California, there is assistance via the California Senior Legal Hotline, which happens to have a designated grandparent project. This non-profit agency recognized the need in this area and through funding from state and federal grants they are able to provide free legal advice by phone and email to California grandparents.

There are few county Superior Courts that provide grandparent visitation forms. This is a problem because without this form, another form must be substituted and modified. Then additional paperwork is necessary to supplement, these are called pleadings. For instance, a form used during a dissolution proceeding for child custody and visitation will be changed by inserting grandparent instead of parent. In California I know of only three counties with the actual grandparent forms, Sacramento, Orange and Riverside. Our organization introduced the ones for Orange, and the ones used in Riverside aren't actually an adopted numbered form, somehow they made up their own.

When a grandparent files a petition PRO PER, they have an easier time when forms are available, otherwise they hit a snag and must rely on a paralegal for help when forms require doctoring. And when an attorney is used, the cost goes up because they spend more time creating a new form with additional paperwork.

Whether or not an attorney is on the case, a packet of forms are necessary, and that's just the beginning. Additionally, grandparents are required to either write their own declaration if they are Pro-Per or present the facts to the attorney, who will edit the information in proper legal format. Building a case requires diligence and cooperation from the client. One of the most important aspects of your case will be proving, or documenting, a pre-existing bond with the grandchild.

Here are the three important additions to any petition packet:

DECLARATION

A declaration is your story about your relationship with your grandchild, why it's important to sustain it and what led to the lost access. The declaration should be short and concise including the relevant facts. It reports the truth as you see it and does not include harsh judgments or denigration of the parent(s). Rambling on about the fitness of the caregiver or third party gossip statements will be frowned upon by a judge. Keep it short, as judges most likely will not read a large file. The length should not exceed four pages, and if the child is young, say, under five, then it only makes sense that the amount of content will be less.

* example: Ch. 11

DATE LOG

All grandparents, whether or not they are facing litigation should keep some sort of journal or calendar. It's not just a negative precaution but can be a reminder of fond memories and shared moments in time.

I suggest marking down significant days that have been spent with the child. When grandparents baby-sit they should make note of it on a calendar. The holidays, the birthdays are pretty easy to keep track of, where and how they were celebrated.

For court cases, include a time-line of specific dates as proof that the grandparent and grandchild spent time together and developed a relationship. Once again, this needs to be edited into a clear and organized format. Don't list all 365 days for each year, instead combine into weeks or months with a highlight of special events. For instance, 2000-2001, the child lived in my home, and during 2001 perhaps the visits were monthly; condense and combine, keeping it under two pages.

* example: Ch.11

PHOTOGRAPHS

This is the most important documentation to be included in your petition packet. Presenting a visual documentation of your relationship with a grandchild cannot be disputed. The pictures speak for themselves. A picture is worth a thousand words.

Similar to the date log, keep it streamlined. Include the least amount of information that will tell the story. Which means go back through every photo taken of you and the child since birth and select the most relevant ones. The idea is to show that you were in the child's life from the beginning and were a consistent presence throughout.

Depending on the age of the child, include no more than ten pages. I suggest using 8 ½ by 11 sheets with three or four photos per page, one side only. You will need to arrange them on the page, adding dates and make at least four copies, one for the judge, one for the clerk of the court, one for opposing counsel and one for yourself and your counsel.

 example: Ch. 11

To summarize, in addition to all pertinent forms (examples Ch. 11) required for grandparent visitation petition forms packet which are about eight, a formal declaration, a date log and photo log should be included. If your attorney doesn't suggest the additional documentation, then either insist on their inclusion or find another attorney.

When filling out the petition, there is a section designated to specific time requests for visitation, always ask for more. In this case quantity trumps quality.

In lieu of court, private mediators are another alternative, some have paralegal backgrounds some have law degrees and prices very similar to attorney fees. On the positive side court costs are saved by going this route. This of course must be agreed upon by all parties.

A couple of more points about settling and mediation. When a court case is filed there is always room for a settlement between parties., often cases are settled on the courthouse steps. And in some states, such as California it is mandatory that in custody and visitation cases that both parties attend court appointed mediation, not the same as private. Court appointed mediation occurs in the family law center of the court and is conducted by in house counselors, at no charge to the parties. The mediator is required to send a report to the judge with the final outcome of the meeting and because of confidentiality ethics specifics about content is not included. If an agreement is reached, then the case is settled, filed and closed, otherwise the process continues with the mediation becoming nothing more than a formality.

If more grandparents clogged the courts, one impact may be to balance out the inequities that currently exist in grandparents' rights. The more grandparents exercise their legal rights, the more respect and understanding we bring to the issue of the importance of the grandparent-grandchild bond. Attention is then given to the fact that it is becoming a growing social problem, (kind of like divorce) if this many folks are clogging the courts.

Chapter 7

Attorneys Speak

Virginia Cornwell, Esq. family law attorney Columbus, outlines the Supreme Court Case on her website:www.cornwell-law.com

Once upon a time there was a U.S. Supreme Court case called Troxel v. Granville, 530 U.S. 57 (2000). The state of Washington used to have a statute that permitted any person to apply for visitation with a child at any time. The Troxels applied for visitation with the daughters of their deceased son. After many appeals, the case reached the U.S. Supreme Court. The U.S. Supreme Court found that that the Washington statute was overly broad, and violated the mother's constitutional due process right to the care, custody and control of her children. In support of their decision, the U.S. Supreme Court noted that the Washington statute had a requirement that the parent be found unfit AND the statute (and the Washington courts) gave no special weight to the wishes of the parent. Pursuant to Parham v. J.R. 442 U.S. 584, there is a presumption that a fit parent acts in the best interest of their child. The Supreme Court went on to say that the problem was not so much that the court intervened, but that it gave no special weight to wishes of the parents.

Law Offices of Virginia Cornwell

603 E. Town Street

Columbus, OH 43215

(614) 225-9316 43215 (614) 225-9316

Attorney Connie Powell provides insight into the Washington State status.

Troxel v. Granville, 530 U.S. 57, 120 S.Ct. 2054, 147 L.Ed.2d 49 (2000) provides a strict rule for grandparents in the state of Washington. Since Troxel, the Washington courts have decided numerous cases which carve out various exceptions and then seemingly narrowing the gap.

Unfortunately,this has led to more confusion for grandparents rights.

Further complications arise by litigation brought from family units which are changing shape in our country. For instance, it took numerous years to the change our laws from the concept of "it takes a village to raise a child" to the more nuclear parenting aspect set by precedence in the 1970's. With the family makeup changing so dramatically today from one set of parents with the right to parent back to the expansion of the definition of families (parents, step-parents, grandparents), our laws are slow to react.

Powell explains her position since the statutes were ruled unconstitutional.

"Frustrating to the extent that I am hamstrung by laws that are not expanding quickly enough to keep up with the true definition of what we call family. Frustrated that we as gp are not provided an opportunity to maintain relationships due to a clear rule that is not always in the best interests of those children which should be the standard. "

" I do still have gp calling. We will continue to chip away until the exceptions, which should be carved on a case by case fact basis, become based on the reality that we should be adding to a child's structure rather than taking away a prime source. I am not saying that every grandparent is a prime source or even that gp visitation or a relationship is even in a child's best interest. That is why a best interest standard should be considered. However, a hard and fast rule that eliminates grandparent rights altogether is too sweeping to cover each family's case and thus should be decided on that case by case basis. "

"Grandparents are realizing that deep legal loss and therefore I believe are not fighting the fight as much. This is of concern and I would like to assist in creating gp exceptions and rules in the proper scenarios. "

Connie L. Powell

Connie L. Powell & Associates, PS

Attorneys at Law

1316 W. Dean

Spokane, Wa 99201

(509) 325-4828

Michael Goldberg, Esq., family law attorney in Chicago supports the idea of uniform national grandparent laws.

I have a significant state-wide grandparent visitation practice in Illinois. In 2002, I argued a case to the Illinois Supreme Court, invalidating the Grandparent Visitation Act in effect at that time. After that case, I wrote the new Grandparent Visitation Act, which has been in effect since 2005. From time to time I am retained in other states to represents grandparents who are seeking court-ordered visitation.

It is my opinion that children are harmed when each state has its own standard for granting third-party visitation. Children would benefit from a uniform application of visitation laws, no matter which state they live in.

IT is beyond dispute that our population is aging, and that the traditional make up of the nuclear family has evolved in the past few decades. Children are forming meaningful relationships with family members other than their biological mother and father. In fact, grandparents (along with other family members) often account for a significant amount of the care for children.

I would be very interested to give more detailed opinions on this topic, either in writing or in person.

Michael K. Goldberg

Goldberg Law Group

120 South Riverside Plaza, Suite 1675

Chicago, IL 60606

(312) 930-5600 ext. 15, (312) 735-1023 cell

mkgoldberg@gf-lawoffice.com

. . . .

Jeff Stivers, Esq. discusses Cal. Family Code: 3104, transcribed from a videotaped interview.

The three requirements that a grandparent has to go through when there is a divorce that has already taken place, and the grandparents are looking for some sort of visitation. The first thing is to show a bond, in other words show that there was a pre-existing relationship with the grandchild and that it would be in the best interest of the child to continue that relationship. If the grandparent does not have a bond, then they have no rights; there has to be a bond created to secure rights. For example if there is a situation where the mom is pregnant and your are going to be a new grandparent but you haven't actually me that child yet: no rights, you have to show a pre-existing bond in order to make it keep going. If the grandparent can show the pre-existing bond then they move onto the next prong, which is a balancing test where the court weighs what is in the best interest of the child versus the parent's right to exercise their authority. The courts will look at why is the parent exercising that parental authority to deny that visitation. In reality the court wants to see a good strong reason, such as the grandparent physically abused the child or had a substance abuse problem and so on. But if the parent doesn't have a big issue like that, then the best interest of the child is going to outweigh that right to be with the grandparent. Because it definitely is in the best interest if there are no other issues, to have more family in their life and to have as much love as possible. So, if a grandparent can get over that hurdle, then the last hurdle, which is the most confusing, 3104 (f). This states that there is a rebuttable presumption that the grandparent visitation is not in the child's best interest if one parent doesn't agree that visitation should be granted. So, once again there is a rebuttable presumption that if one parent says no, the court should listen to that and say no. What this means is that the rebuttable presumption is rebuttable. In other words when the judge starts his analysis on this particular issue, he's going to think that the parent is right. It's as though he is saying," I'm going to start my thinking with the fact that the parent is right, and now lets see if the grandparents can rebut that presumption and prove, no that the parent is wrong and it's actually in the child's best interest to still maintain visitation with "me" the grandparent. Overcoming all three hurdles, are required to secure visitation rights and the bottom line is proof of the bond.

Last, grandparents need to be aware that when pursuing

these cases that child support and attorney fees are a factor.

Jeffrey N. Stivers, Esq.

Law Office of Jeffrey N. Stivers

28202 Cabot Road, Third Floor

Laguna Niguel, CA 92677

949-364-1199 ph   http://www.jeffreystiverslaw.com

. . . .

Link Schwartz, Esq. Los Angeles family law attorney wants increased awareness.

I ALSO BELIEVE THAT TWO THINGS HAVE TO HAPPEN: We need more cases, more appeals and someone working diligently with the legislature for CHANGE!!!

IT BECOMES MORE UPSETTING TO ME EVERY DAY TO HEAR ALL OF THE STORIES THAT CROSS MY PATH.

The majority of people who call for help just don't have the money to do it. If I could finance it I really would - I just don't have the funds.

INJUSTICE – INEQUITY-system does not account adequately for this.

HEARTBREAK - rips apart well- bonded families and vital relationships for children.

CASES ARE SEVERELY UNDER REPORTED

MOST OLDER CITIZENS DO NOT HAVE THE FUNDS TO LITIGATE

CHILDREN SUFFER THE MOST

ISSUES OF ABANDONMENT

THIS IS A CRISIS AND NO ONE IS PAYING ATTENTION.

WHY? BECAUSE IT AFFECTS CHILDREN (no voice), and Seniors (who cares?!).

Link K. Schwartz A Law Corporation

1801 Century Park East Suite 1100

Los Angeles, CA 90067 (310) 553-5465

. . . .

Sheryl Edgar, Esq. family law attorney: discusses a portion of Cal. Family code 3104, (5) transcribed from a videotaped interview.

In the legal system today, they carved out a very small area for grandparent –relative visitation. The way they did that is there's a constitution that gives parents autonomy to parent as they wish. The state and government will not interfere with that parenting unless it's essential to the welfare of the minor child to remove that from the parenting. Otherwise the state can't come in your door and tell you how to parent your children. So, it was very difficult for the state to come up with a way to come in your door and tell you the parent that the grandparents are going to have visitation over your objection. That's why the drafting of the law was so difficult. When they drafted the round of California legislation for grandparent visitation under 3104, they put in all these hoops that a grandparent would have to go through. For example as the relationship that is deteriorating between the parents and that the grandparents are the most supportive people during that time. If children are going through a divorce and the family Is separating, they wanted a place where the grandparents are still there for the children and could be there during that process and that neither parent could exclude the grandparents, so that's one way the grandparents could in the door.

The other way is if only one parent objected to the visitation, then the grandparent could join the parent that agreed with the visitation and ask the court for visitation.

Another circumstance is when the child created a bond with the grandparent, similar to Susan's case, and the parents split up and after a period of time the mother remarried and the new husband adopted the child. The way the law was written at the time it completely severs the rights as a grandparent because the lineage is severed. The father of the child's rights become terminated when they sign off on adoption, and the new stepfather adopted the child and became the father, therefore there is no grandparent in that case. The mother of the stepfather would be replaced in that position.

What Susan Hoffman set out to do is determine what would need to change in the law so that an adoption would not sever grandparent's rights to visitation with a child with whom a bond had developed. I am proud to say that is exactly what Susan's done, and now all grandparents will benefit from the fact that they could have had a four year, five year ten year relationship with a grandchild and the acts of the parents will not be able to sever that relationship.

Sheryl L. Edgar, Esq.

Senior Partner

CENTER FOR CHILDREN & FAMILY LAW

1111 W. Chapman Ave.

Orange, CA 92868

(714) 937-1234

Chapter 8

GET ON WITH LIFE

A Grandparent will never get over the heartbreak of losing access to a grandchild, they can however, take steps to get on with life. You don't get over it, but you get on with it. Getting on with life has individual meaning, for some you never stop grieving but somehow learn to live with the loss.

It requires the ability to compartmentalize our minds. You just take the pain and park it for a while so that way you can do other things. If you don't then it renders you powerless to live life as a productive human being. Obsessing about the "what ifs", and the "if onlys" is counterproductive, it's in the past. Finding joy and happiness in other ways is what it's all about.

We love our grandchildren deeply and think about them everyday, but they are a *part* of our life and not our entire life. Anything or anyone in which we become attached, causes us to be powerless. Waiting is the lowest form of life's participation. We know that someday we will be re-united with our grandchild, but we don't know exactly when. For some it may be when they are eighteen or at least old enough to make their own decisions, but you can't put your life on hold until then. This is about taking care of ourselves first.

How do we do that?

JOURNAL

Writing to our grandchild is a way of staying connected. You don't have to be a professional writer to keep a journal. Tell the child about your life, what you do everyday, favorite foods, hobbies, work and share your emotions, thoughts and feelings. Some of what you write will be sad for sure, but it doesn't all have to be a sob story.

A missing grandchild has already lost the day to day interaction along with pieces of history that are a part of having a relationship with a grandparent. Give them some of that history back by writing about yourself and let them get to know you.

Another way to journal is to create a website about the child, Nikki from Ohio did this. Although it didn't score points with the already angry parents, Nikki felt doing nothing wouldn't have made a difference. The parents are in another state and have made it clear that they will not change their mind.

Designing a website in honor of a grandchild should be a good thing as long as boundaries are not crossed and the theme remains in the spirit in which it is intended, to love, honor and communicate in a special way. Be careful about using photos of the children, permission may be necessary.

WORK

If you are not already working, then find something to do that you enjoy and hopefully can get paid for doing it. If you like to be around people then perhaps a hostess job, sales clerk, receptionist, anything that makes you feel productive and worthwhile, and makes you feel like you matter. Besides, work keeps you young.

HEALTH

Part of health is exercise and it can be a saving grace when we are feeling low. In fact maybe that is the best time to get moving, when you least feel like it. There is nothing better than that endorphin high.

Getting outdoors and breathing fresh air stimulates our senses. Taking a walk, riding a bike are great examples of the importance of moving and pumping blood into the heart. Find a walking buddy, so it becomes a shared experience, something you both can look forward to doing and make one another accountable. Join a walking group most cities have them. Soon you will look forward to walking. If you can't always go with someone then load up the ITUNES or a favorite radio station, or how about just enjoy the quiet time with your thoughts. Sometime I get my best ideas during an outdoor walk.

Take a class, Yoga, Zumba, spin, sculpt, Pilates, any kind

of aerobic activity to get your heart rate up, work up a sweat and raise endorphin level. You will meet new people and begin to look forward to going.

Eat healthy and avoid alcohol and drugs. Numbing the pain with unhealthy substances will only add to the stress and increase depression.

That includes food, filling the void with food is just as bad as numbing the pain with drugs and alcohol. TV isn't so good either, talk about a mind numbing experience, that and a bowl of vanilla fudge swirl should be a mood elevator for sure. I don't think so.

I am not saying that you have to surround yourself with people, being alone is great, however there are so many other activities to engage oneself in besides unhealthy food and crappy TV. How about reading?

There is nothing quite like visiting a library or a book store to restore one's soul, and then actually losing oneself in a novel. Well, there's nothing quite like it. Reading is an action packed experience television is passive. We are participating in the activity, a huge difference between mindless staring at the tube.

HOBBY

Finding something fun to do is a form of play, something adults forget to do. There is an influx of classes for just about everything imaginable.

Find something interesting to do and go have fun.

Examples:

Knitting: it's really popular everyone is wearing those long neck scarves.

Art: painting, sculpting, crafting classes can be found just about everywhere, or buy a book and teach yourself.

Golf: get out there and walk eighteen holes and take in the surroundings while playing the game of life.

Woodworking: therapeutic for sure, it's all about the process, and sometime the finished product.

Sailing: the wind, the sea, the beauty and calm that the ocean sometimes arouses in anyone who has gone sailing.

Collecting: antiques, shells, frogs, doorknobs, what-knots, it doesn't matter as long as you're having fun.

VOLUNTEER

The opportunities are endless. What better way to get out of yourself than to do something for someone else? It's truly the best therapy of all.

There are so many who are worse off that you. If working with children somehow fulfills that emptiness, start researching those opportunities.

Children are hungry everywhere, children need mentors,

caregivers, tutors, love and attention. If it's too painful to be around kids, then lend assistance to adult programs, or environmental issues, law enforcement, travel to disaster affected regions, god knows they could use the help.

Finding a place to lend your services is not difficult they are all over the Internet, newspapers, TV and throughout our communities.

One person giving time can make a difference.

SCHOOL

You are never too old to learn. Go back to school, whether college or independent classes, do it. Learn to speak a foreign language, operate a computer, photography, writing, psychology, math, English, anything, just challenge yourself. Colleges and Universities are courting the return of seniors to the classroom.

TRAVEL

So much to see and such a terrific way to enrich our lives, learning about new places, near and far. We all have budgets to live by and traveling is expensive, but if it is within our means it offers rewards beyond our imagination. My friend, Bart, has a curiosity beyond belief, so much so that he visited 320 countries within about 13 years. He is among a select group, but he accomplished a goal where the bar was set very high. You don't have to go to those extremes; there are new places to explore right in our own backyard so to speak. Traveling to new cities and states can be an eye opener, even if it's a day trip from the suburbs of Orange County to China town in downtown Los Angeles, it's still a new experience visiting a different culture.

EMOTIONAL HEALTH

How about working on your emotional health? Most people don't participate in their own recovery. It's not easy and takes much work and self- introspection. Making an effort to become more enlightened, more patient, kind, thoughtful, honest, tactful and communicative is not a bad goal to have. How about learning how to accept yourself. How about learning how to stop blaming others, or being the victim. What about keeping agreements and developing a strong sense of integrity.

Seeing a counselor or therapist is one solution to addressing the emotional baggage. Reading self -help books works for some. Connecting with others experiencing similar circumstances such as in a support group is also effective.. Cultivating social relationships period is a vital part of self- growth and sustains emotional well being.

Spending some alone time isn't so bad either. We all need to re-charge now and again. Some swear by meditation, prayer and or spiritual healing. You know what they say, be your own best friend. It works!

The mind body connection needs to be treated as a whole and not individually. It's not the crazy ones who seek therapy it's the ones who want to be better, stronger and whole individuals. To be the best they can be. To evolve.

Chapter 9

MAKE A DIFFERENCE

One person can make a difference. Start taking action to change what you're unhappy about. Rather than complaining, do something about it. Big stuff or small, making the effort to create change where you want it, empowers you.

I chose to change something really big: the law. Not everyone will be able to change a law, as I did. It's just not realistic; the stars must be aligned so to speak, all the cogs must connect. The entire system must work, and everything must fall into place in order to create the end result, a law. It is a difficult endeavor requiring many players.

For example, AB 2517 (2006) had all the right ingredients so it would successfully pass legislation and become law.

It started with an idea I had: "Grandparents must be granted standing in court to file a petition for grandparent visitation following a stepparent adoption." When my son consented to the stepparent adoption of his son, the biological mom and new dad reneged on a previous verbal agreement to allow me continued contact with my grandson, Jacob. In the eyes of the court, once the biological dad relinquished his parental rights, my rights as a grandparent also disappeared. I was no longer recognized as Jacob's grandma; I was stripped of that title by an existing law that didn't make sense. So, this is how I came up with the idea, it became personal. At least at first. More on this later.

It took me two times to get it right. The first time I wasn't organized enough and I picked the wrong lawmaker. You gotta have an author (lawmaker) to carry forward your idea. Plus I was a little too desperate.

The second go around, the desperation was gone which is what I meant by it not being as personal. I was actually seeing Jacob once again after a three year hiatus because the adoptive dad contacted me. Another side story: he allegedly brought me back into Jacob's life because he said it was in Jacob's best interest, along with an admission of guilt for cutting me off the first time. It turns out I allowed myself to be a pawn in that situation. My return to Jacob's life was about his retaliation toward the mom. In the end his actions of taking grandma away, bringing her back and then taking her away again would impact Jacob's and my relationship. The last time that we were together was June 18, 2006. The parents' actions caused me tremendous heartache, but what they did to Jacob is unforgivable.

Getting back to my reasons for sponsoring a bill, at the time, January of 2006, even though I was seeing Jacob, I was continuing to work with other grandparents who were going through the same thing. I never forgot how it felt to lose visitation and vowed to continue to help others and never give up the fight. It was now for the greater good.

There was a new legislator who replaced the termed out Ken Maddox, whom I'd worked with previously. The new lawmaker's name was Assemblyman Van Tran of Costa Mesa. On a whim, without expectations but with a feeling of confidence and neutrality, I set up an appointment to meet with the Assemblyman. One possible stumbling block -- I wasn't a constituent. Some legislators won't even talk to you unless you live in their district. I suppose that it was my relationship with Tran's office manager, Trish Zanella, who stayed on to work with Tran that created a certain level of comfort for me about returning to the familiar office. She was also a grandmother and had shared that she had once been estranged from her grandchildren. We established a connection from the very beginning and have been friends ever since.

Assemblyman Tran was immediately on board without hesitation. We had a brief meeting discussing my idea for a bill to help grandparents and he did inquire about my residency, which didn't disqualify me or my idea to become the sponsor of a bill. So, now we had ingredient number one and two, idea and someone to introduce it.

The third ingredient is getting support for the bill so that it will be approved first by the two Judiciary Committees of both branches of the California Legislature and then it must be voted on by the entire Assembly and Senate in order to be passed. Preparing for this final vote is called lobbying and it takes much hard work which is why professional lobbyists make the big bucks. It's a full time job for sure and requires tenacity, commitment and persistence.

You are working against the clock and a strict calendar set in stone. I quit my job and devoted every waking hour of every day for 8 months to see it through.

Once the idea is accepted by the legislator the bill is drafted by legislative council, and from there it is introduced by the author. Then the lobbying begins by the legislative office and the sponsors of the bill, in this case me. This means that I had to locate constituents in every district of the state so that they could contact their legislators with a letter of support for the bill. The key legislators to be contacted at first are the Judiciary Committee members of both houses, because the bill has to get passed there in order to go before the general Assembly and Senate, so even though all 120 legislators needed to be contacted, there is an order of importance.

My law had everything going for it, which means it was smooth sailing throughout. The law remained on the CONSENT CALENDAR throughout the legislative process, which means there was no opposition, therefore putting it on the fast track. This rarely happens; very few bills are afforded this status. AB 2517 breezed through the legislative process with all 120 legislators in approval and zero opposition and was signed into law by Governor Schwarzeneggar in August 2006.

Every individual has the ability and the right to contact their district legislators with comments and grievances. They work for you, not the other way around. It is also everyone's responsibility to know who their representatives are.

Another means of being heard is to form a united front. Gather other grandparents together to form a support group. How do you do that? The first step is to find a place that can accommodate a group and not charge for the use. My group is a nonprofit, so there is never a charge. The second step is to run an ad in the calendar/event section of the local paper, put up flyers and generally spread the word in order to attract attendees.

Your group could be a combination of support, education, and activism with a purpose for change. Change comes in all forms: change in behavior brought about by group suggestion can make a difference, as does lending support by just listening to someone else; walking into a support group where others are experiencing a similar problem and realizing that you are no longer alone, can make a difference. We all have the power to make a difference in someone else's life and although it may seem small, it counts. Lending support by letting other people know they are not alone is making a difference.

Forming a support group is reciprocal. You receive help and you give help. Everyone involved makes a difference in each other's life.

Support groups on behalf of grandparent visitation issues do not have to be passive. Fundraising events are crucial to increasing awareness; contacting the media is another way of getting stories told. Marches, rallies, conferences, walks, runs, sales, events of any kind as way to speak up and speak out is all fair game. Just do something.

Chapter 10

A Compendium Of Grand Magazine Articles

Not So Grand

When grandparent visitation rights go wrong

By Susan Hoffman

Dear Susan,

After my daughter Sara tragically died in an automobile accident, her former husband, with whom she shared custody of their two children, Maura, age 6, and Matthew, age 4, moved with them to Spokane, Washington, from California. My husband and I had been an integral part of our grandchildren's lives since the day they were born.

We were only able to see them once before Joe left with them, 30 days after Sara's death. We had the children for a day at an amusement center; we were so optimistic about sharing their future. Joe fooled us. He told us, "The kids had a great time, and I may be needing your help in the future." Joe said we would be an important part of their lives, but all the while he was planning his move. He left without a word to any of our family, and we had had no contact, even by telephone since October 20, 2006. The heartache was more than we could stand. After many months of unanswered emails, letters and phone calls we decided to take legal action; that was November 2007, and we are still embroiled in the fight of our lives because of manipulative delays caused by the father.

— *Heartbroken Grandma Julie*

Susan responds: This example of denied grandparent access may be the most tragic of all scenarios. These children lost not only a parent but also an entire side of their family. I wish I could say that this is an unusual situation, but sadly it is not. Somewhere along the way it has been lost that grandparents are a crucial resource for families and that children deserve to have all the love they can get. When children are unreasonably denied access to grandparents with whom they have bonded, the children lose part of their past and grandparents lose their future. Children are often treated as property with little concern for their wants, needs and emotional welfare. When their liberty interests are violated, it is the grandparents who end up becoming their voices. Although these issues are referred to as grandparent rights, in reality it is the right of a child to remain connected to grandparents.

Grandparent rights are not "automatic" but merely give standing in a court of law, which means grandparents may petition the court for visitation with a grandchild when they find themselves entangled with visitation issues that can only be solved in court.

The grandparent visitation rights movement is directed toward protecting and preserving that part of a child's extended family. It is an ongoing struggle of individuals promoting the preservation of the family unit by influencing legislation and the public. *May- June 2010*

Banned Forever!

"One slip of the tongue cost us our granddaughter"

By Susan Hoffman

Dear Susan,

On the surface our life looked perfect, but behind closed doors our family was falling apart. A feeling of emptiness and heartache consumes us because of our lost access to our little granddaughter. Not a day goes by when I don't think of her. My DIL [daughter-in-law] Beth and I used to be so close: She and I would make tufa pots in her yard, go to nurseries looking for plants to put in them, show and sell our final products locally. We had a lot of fun. She and my son lived nearby, making get-togethers all the more convenient. They came to Mexico for visits, skied in Colorado with us, ate dinners out; and then we shopped for baby clothes together.

One day everything changed. I still play it over and over

in my head trying to figure out what exactly happened to completely sever all ties between us. What did I say or do in the backyard that summer day to make her and my son so mad that now we are forever banned from their lives and from our young granddaughter?

Our calls and e-mails went unanswered, so on Easter morning a few weeks later, my husband and I went to the house to deliver a basket for our granddaughter. When our son answered the door, he was fuming as he glared at us and then refused to accept the Easter basket. He admonished us for coming over unannounced and told us to stay away. We were in shock.

From that day on there was no further communication from our son or his wife. We didn't give up though; we sent heartfelt letters, "thinking of you" cards, gifts, and even hired a mediator — nothing worked. The gifts and cards were never acknowledged, nor were they returned.

It has been almost three years since we have had contact of any kind, which amounts to almost half of our granddaughter's life since we have held her, played with her or talked to her. We sent Presley a birthday card last week, but who knows if they even opened it. One time I saw her from a distance as she came out of her school; it was wonderful to see her, but it made me sad.

Coincidentally, we live just three blocks from them, but

it may as well be 3,000 miles. There have been a few awkward moments when we have passed them in our car or on bikes, not sure what to do — we just waved and kept going. Our reasoning is that if they don't see us as a threat, maybe they will let us back into their lives. That is our hope.

Keeping up a façade can be exhausting. One day my neighbor asked, "Where is your son? I haven't seen him in a while." I reluctantly admitted that somehow Dave has the notion that we did not accept his wife into the family and therefore, decided to distance himself; we can only ascertain this information secondhand, as he no longer speaks to us. My neighbor was not shocked: He then shared his story about how his daughter had not been around for 15 years. He went on to say the daughter wrote them once stating that she would reconsider allowing them back into her life and let them see the grandkids if they sent $50,000.

Susan, at first it was embarrassing to tell anyone, especially since I thought that I was the only one this was happening to. As time went by, it seemed everyone had a similar story. I no longer felt alone."
— *Alienated Grandma Laura*

Susan responds: Laura's experience is a heartbreaker, and she's right: It's happening to families everywhere. Talking about it brings great relief to disenfranchised grandparents. Talking about it to other grandparents experiencing similar circumstances can be a godsend. Once we learn that we are not alone and that this is happening to many others, then we no longer have to endure the suffering in silence. It lightens the load and lessens the stress.

It is humiliating to admit that our own children can be so cruel and that they are treating us with such contempt to the point that we have been locked out of their lives. We all want to be proud parents and then look forward to enjoying the rewards that go along with grandparenthood—and when it all crumbles, then we ask ourselves: "Where did I go wrong as a parent?" While it is natural to blame ourselves, at some point we need to let go of the guilt we harbor and realize it is the adult children who have made these choices and may very well need to take ownership for their behavior.

Visitation issues hover over many families and sometimes never surface, and this may be attributable to the temperament of personalities or perceptive intervention of those heading it off at the pass before it becomes a problem. My friend refers to her DIL as "THE LAW." She saw it coming and has taken preventative measures by adapting her own behavior so she can remain within the acceptable boundaries. This may sound rigid, but that is the world we live in; if grandparents want a free pass, then they must follow the rules.

All it takes is a slip of the tongue before there is an unintended consequence, and suddenly a switch goes off and grandparents find themselves on the outside looking in. There is no room for egos or the need to be right. The parents hold the keys to the kingdom, and they are in control. Without them, there is no visitation, especially when the family is living in an "intact" situation (such as Laura's). Although every state does have grandparent visitation statutes, few include the "intact" criterion, (standing to file a petition when the parents are married and living together). In these situations, grandparents must rely on their own resources, including support from others rather than legal avenues.

"Unreasonably denied" visitation has become a growing social problem affecting many families. Everyone suffers, especially the child who doesn't understand and feels abandoned when the attachment has been broken, along with a loss of affection. It is a form of emotional child abuse, so it is the grandparents, by lending their voices on behalf of a child, who are finally speaking out and setting themselves and all of the skeletons in the closet free. *July - Aug 2010*

Temper, Temper

A grandchild needs to know you'll fight for them

By Susan Hoffman

Dear Susan,

It all started when I flipped the boyfriend off.

My daughter and her son came to live with me shortly after his birth; she and the bio dad never married, and he wasn't interested in being a parent. We were one big happy family for seven years, until I did a very bad thing and gave my daughter's new boyfriend 'the finger.'

Tiffany began dating Donato, a hairdresser with an ego the size of Texas and a strong desire to control. Upon meeting him and seeing the changes in my daughter's attitude, I voiced my concern and brutally honest opinion including a strong dislike toward him, to my daughter. She told him what I had said, and the next thing I know, he's on my doorstep yelling at me. He never gave me a chance to speak, and then as he was driving away, that is when I gave him the finger. I know — stupid and immature.

That evening when my daughter returned, she was fuming, threatening to have nothing to do with me ever again; I relented, dialed his number, leaving a voice message that I was sorry. He did not respond.

The next day Tiffany packed her bags and those of Trevor

and moved out of my house and into Donato's. My fault — now my home, my life, felt empty.

It has been three years since they moved out and three years that I have gone from seeing Trevor every day and helping raise him, to seeing him less than one hour a year if I'm lucky. I can't believe it has been that long; I never thought it would be permanent. I guess I still don't, judging by my non-action.

I was cut out of both of their lives and forced to comply with my daughter's "don't call us, we'll call you" law. She made it clear: "Don't even try our number or e-mail; they have been changed, and I don't want you harassing us by dropping by the house." I didn't go quietly; I tried everything to make amends. Nothing worked. Once, I attended his school's open house and got reprimanded for that.

The holidays came and went; all I could do is wait and hope that she would come around. Oh and sometimes, she would throw me a crumb, which was better than nothing. I secretly hoped that the relationship between she and Donato would end, and then she and Trevor would come back.

Upon advisement from my support group, I finally consulted with a family law attorney specializing in grandparent visitation rights, and she informed me that I did have standing in court to file a petition for visitation because of the pre-existing relationship and strong bond that Trevor and I had shared since he had lived with me. I wrote the retainer check, signed the contract and never went back.

I stopped going to the support group meetings, stopped calling the coach for strategies, and let my pending lawsuit remain in limbo.

I wait and hope. Maybe my daughter will come back with my grandson.

— *Wishing & Hoping Denise*"

Susan responds: Denise came to me obsessed that her daughter had helplessly fallen into the powers of Donato's control and that she no longer had the free will to make her own choices. She was so focused on the "whys" that she failed to see the true harmful result of her daughter's behavior: the child's welfare.

Everyone lost sight of the relationship between the grandparent and grandchild. Grandma did a bad thing; mom retaliated, compounding the situation. No matter what is going on between the parents and grandparents, the child should not be the loser. What is truly sad is that this grandmother didn't take action to protect the relationship, which would have been to maintain a consistent time allotment with her grandson, with whom a strong bond had developed. The grandmother had the opportunity to provide a balance. This child lost the stability of his home life and the affection and nurturing that his grandmother provided. Yet, the grandmother is in such denial that she fails to see that when someone shows you who they are, believe them. Including your own flesh and blood. Even if her daughter eventually "comes around," what about the time that has been lost?

When the only alternative to remain in a grandchild's life, best interests considered, is through litigation; then time is of the essence. Court procedures are lengthy, and time in a child's life is critical; besides, judges question delays in filing. It is all about the bond: the presence of strength resides in consistency and time.

A child needs to know that a grandparent is willing to fight for them! *Sept - Oct 2010*

Blowing the Whistle

What's the price of trying to protect a grandchild?

By Susan Hoffman

Dear Susan,

As a grandparent, if you had found out that your grandchild had been living with a parent and stepparent who were engaging in a sleazy lifestyle and allowing friends who were also involved to be around the child, would you have attempted to get guardianship? My daughter and her husband are a part of the adult entertainment industry, including stripping and nude photography in magazines and on the Internet and who knows what else.

Sometimes I get so discouraged.... Had I done nothing and something happened to my grandchild, I wouldn't be able to live with myself, yet since I have tried to protect them, I have become alienated and have hardly seen Hayley at all.

We did what we thought was right by calling CPS and then filing for guardianship, which we soon learned was unrealistic, because most of the activities in the adult entertainment profession are legal, therefore not a reason to remove a child from the home, unless they are proven to be a participant.

The CPS investigation found no just cause, and we dropped the guardianship and instead filed a grandparent visitation petition, which seemed the only way to remain in our grandchild's life at this point. Our action resulted in consequences.

Our daughter used Hayley to hurt us by keeping her from us. How can a mother force a 5-year-old child to sever a relationship out of spite? How can she cause a child emotional pain and the court not see that as emotional abuse?

There are days that it takes all that I have to keep it together; I miss Hayley so much and the special bond that we share. I was even in the delivery room when she was born. The thought of what they must be telling her, or the way she must be feeling, kills me.

When things really started falling apart, my husband and I did some serious back-peddling, with lots of "eating crow" in an attempt to remain in our daughter's and granddaughter's lives. After unsuccessfully trying to work something out with our daughter, we decided to go forward with our case, and the judge awarded us temporary visitation of four hours twice monthly until a final judgment was rendered. Although it is a far cry from what we once had, it is better than nothing.

I see clear evidence that Hayley is being told what she can and cannot say to us. She'll catch herself and change what she was going to say. She keeps asking to spend the night, and is disappointed that our visits are so short.

As our case progresses, things are coming out, including pertinent information about Hayley's emotional well being based on a court-appointed therapist's evaluation. Her observation reinforced what we knew: that Hayley had been anxious and depressed during the five months that we had been separated and that as a result of the visits she expressed happiness.

The court-appointed therapist's evaluation carried much weight with the judge and therefore was the deciding factor in awarding us a permanent visitation order. Given the circumstances that this child has to live with, her time with us is not enough, but it is a start and the only way to watch over her. There are occasional slipups with Hayley confiding in us, which cause alarms to go off within us, and confirm that we must keep vigilance over her well being.

— *Ever Vigilant Granny Gail*

Susan responds: A couple of issues here: "blowing the whistle" and "persistence." What is one to do? Report the alleged wrongdoing? In other words, err on the side of caution at the risk of alienation from parents and denied access to the grandchild? Or ignore? Or do something in between?

Grandparents have assumed the role of protector, overseer of grandchildren, and within that innate role they risk opposition from parents with the threat of being cut off if they express their concerns when they observe something out of sync with a potential harm that could jeopardize the welfare of the child.

The child's safety and security comes first, and when the parents aren't accountable, the grandparents are left with the responsibility of advocate. In Gail's case, there is no right or wrong answer. She and her husband acted in what they thought was the best interest of the child based on the information that they had. Sometimes emotions blur facts, especially where a child is concerned; however, if fact gathering is at all possible (the element of danger notwithstanding), then stepping back and doing the homework may be more effective.

The second issue, persistence, is vital when it comes to watching over a child. Grandparents can provide the "balance" so necessary in the achievement of the child's emotional well being by sticking close by. Unless the grandparents are willing to fight the fight in order to remain close to the grandchild, the child will never know the opposite of a dysfunctional home life. Gail and her husband hung in there throughout the exhaustive court/legal process, endured animosity and suffered extreme debt, all because they believed that their granddaughter deserved to be treated like she mattered. *Nov - Dec 2010*

Reinventing the Holidays

A grieving grandmother finds her own way to survive the holidays

By Susan Hoffman

Dear Susan,

There are no signs of a holiday season at my house. There are no decorations, no lights strung outside or in, no wreath, no tree, no music, no holiday parties and no Christmas spirit. I agree that I may fit the "bah-humbug" profile, except for one thing: I do remember my loved ones with gifts.

The joy of Christmas ended for me about five years ago on Christmas Day, as I anxiously awaited the arrival of my 3-year-old grandson to come and spend our first-ever Christmas Day together. I had invited my parents and siblings to share in the celebration of this very special holiday, where we would all be able to finally watch him open his gifts. It always feels more like Christmas having a kid around. Our merriment soon turned to sorrow when my son walked through the door without little Alex. He had accepted the mom's excuse that Alex had suddenly come down with the flu and chalked it up to yet another thwarted visit.

It was more than just one holiday and one day of disappointment. Things never got better. Alex never came back.

His dad's frustration grew to the point that he simply gave up and stopped trying, eventually fading out of the picture entirely, but I kept fighting until I came across an unyielding judge who blocked my access as a result of a long and drawn-out court battle. For me the traditions that go along with the Xmas holidays died that day. I have chosen to reinvent the holidays by eliminating traditions; I can only do what I am comfortable with, and one of those things is to make a charitable contribu-tion to another child in my grandson's name, and this is how I survive an otherwise stressful time.

— *Grandma Scrooge*

Susan responds: It takes a good deal of courage to stop wor-rying about what others think and break away from conforming expectations about the way things are supposed to be. There is no right or wrong way to honor holidays, just as there is no right or wrong coping strategy. We all cope differently, and whatever works for reducing stress is the best Rx.

I don't think this grandmother is being a scrooge, but instead she is taking care of herself. She has painful feelings about holiday time because she associates it with all the unful-filled expectations of spending at least part of the time with her grandchild. She doesn't see the child during holidays or at all, nor is the child allowed to receive her gifts. She has changed her perceptions about how things are supposed to be and has adjusted her behavior to coincide. By eliminating the frills, the decorating, the parties and switching the radio station away from Christmas music, she is protecting herself from sadness and anxiety that brings about stress. She has figured out that these are the stressors that can trigger an undesirable response: depression.

We have to do what is necessary to take care of ourselves especially during holiday time, even if it doesn't fit society's expectations. *Jan - Feb 2011*

Sneaking Around

When it comes to court-ordered visitations, should you follow your heart or your head?

By Susan Hoffman

Dear Susan,

I represented myself in family court, which is known as "pro per," and won my court-ordered visitation with my grandson. I now have 12 hours a month, picking him up from school every other Friday and then spending the afternoon and part of the evening with him before taking him home at 9 p.m. It's not enough for either of us. The problem is now we are sneaking. My grandson calls me in between the court-ordered visits and asks for rides to and from school, especially when it rains. It's so hard, I just can't say no, and sometimes he's calling because he's hungry. The first time he called, it was during our recent rainstorms in California and I didn't think twice, just picked him up and drove him to school. But when his mom (my daughter) found out, she went ballistic and threatened to stop all visits.

It seems so petty that she is making such a big deal out it.

I then explained to my grandson that it's too risky and we will end up losing what we have, but he still begs. He now has me pick him up a block from school and then he lies down on the seat to hide just in case. My head tells me that I am violating a court order and should follow the rules, but my heart tells me to spring into action and face the consequences later. I'm his only support and want to always be there for him.

— *Partner in crime Grandma Delia*

Susan responds: Obtaining a court order for visitation is like having an insurance policy. This grandma is pretty smart to have navigated the system and prevailed in court on her own, an accomplishment to be proud of, for sure. But emotions can overtake common sense and govern our decisions when it comes to answering a grandchild's call for help. We are putty in their hands. It is so tempting to jump in and rescue these kids whenever they call upon us, no matter how small or large the request may be. In Delia's case I reminded her that she has too much at stake and that she should not take the risk of losing her visits when a judge finds her in contempt of not following the order. When I suggested that she buy her grandson an umbrella and some fast-food gift certificates, she laughed and said, "Good idea, I didn't think of that." There is also the possibility that the boy, actually an adolescent, may be playing Grandma Delia? This is not uncommon when adults put kids in the middle. The kids become the ping-pong ball, in this case between mom and grandmom. They are conflicted; they love their parent and grandparent and feel like they are forced to make a choice. Rather than burn either bridge, they learn how to play both sides against the middle as a way of coping.

It could also be that the boy is using the rides as an excuse to spend more time with his grandmother. Perhaps it's his way of rebelling against his mother's authority.

Delia's situation, giving the kid a ride here and there, doesn't appear to be terribly serious on the surface. But what lies under the surface cannot be known. Grandchildren and grandparents should not have to lie and sneak to do what seems like a natural part of life, but there are bound to be unwanted consequences. Sadly, a child's emotional welfare is not a priority for the reporting agencies. The scars from emotional abuse are not visible; therefore, they must not be real. Or are they?

Mar - Apr 2011

My Way or the Highway

To keep the peace — and your grandchild — do you have to be a doormat?

By Susan Hoffman

Dear Susan,

My son and his girlfriend were living with us throughout her pregnancy and until our first grandchild turned 1. I can't say that it was easy, but we made the best of it. Our son, Patrick, worked full time, and Kelly, his girlfriend, lost her receptionist job about halfway through her pregnancy, so she was home a lot. I noticed her mood swings and attributed it to her hormones being out of whack because of her pregnancy, but then it got worse after she gave birth. She was so ugly and hurtful toward my wife and me that nothing ever seemed right.

She got a job so that they could save enough money to move out, and we offered to care for Pat Jr. while they were at work. We did everything for our grandson: food, clothing and shelter, including taking him to his doctor appointments. When Kelly was around, she criticized everything — from the clothes we bought him to the food we gave him. She even accused us of stepping over boundaries by rejecting her authority. If we put him down for his nap too early because he seemed tired, then all hell broke loose. If we fed him the wrong lunch, then she scolded us.

Life became unbearable having her there, so I got angry and told her that we weren't willing to have her live in our house as long as she continued the verbal abuse toward us. The next day she was gone.

Our son and our grandson moved out along with her, and now

he feels conflicted. He has tried to smooth things out, but she won't listen, and he is so proud to be a dad that he can't risk losing his new family.

It has been over two months now, and our calls, emails and texts are not returned. We left messages stating that we just wanted to see our grandson, pick him up and bring him back without any drama or interaction from the mom. Our son called right after they moved out and said she refused to let us see our grandson. She said for us not to come over and to stop calling and messaging. And now, he's not communicating. I don't know what to do anymore — the pain is more than I can endure.

— Enabling grandparents Bob and Teresa

Susan responds: Grandparents Bob and Teresa have every right to expect courteous behavior from anyone living in their home. The problem is that they waited too long to constructively confront the situation. They allowed the problem to percolate by letting the anger build up instead of nipping it in the bud before it got out of hand.

Maybe they had expectations that the son's girlfriend would be grateful to have a roof over her head and built-in babysitters; however, many young parents feel a sense of entitlement when it comes to their parents' (in-laws) support. This is a different generation, and there's a reason it's called the "me" generation: because as their parents, we wanted to make their life easier and better than ours.

When you fail to set boundaries for your grown children or anyone for that matter, they will walk all over you. I understand this is especially difficult when a grandchild is involved because you don't want to rock the boat and lose access. So, how does one set reasonable boundaries for themselves and adhere to them without alienating the violators?

Grandparents do indeed need to take the high road at all times, and set egos aside and even do their share of crow eating, and all on behalf of the child. This can be accomplished with the development of effective communication techniques without feeling like a doormat.

These grandparents over-functioned by doing too much and never asking for a reciprocal living arrangement.

At this point, perhaps the best approach for Bob and Teresa is to send the young couple a brief note apologizing for their angry outburst and offer an olive branch. The other issue to be addressed, the grandparents are expecting to bypass the relationship with the mom and go straight to the grandchild visitation. This rarely happens. If they want to continue a relationship with the grandchild, then the relationship with the parent(s) needs to be cultivated. Parents hold the keys to the kingdom. It's best to always include them and embrace the entire family instead of just the child. *May - June 2011*

Brainwashing Hannah

Emotional abuse leaves scars that may never heal

By Susan Hoffman

Dear Susan,

My daughter and son-in-law are separated, and I am now living with my daughter and granddaughter. I am pleased to say that I have become my granddaughter's caregiver when my daughter is working. Everyone gets along well, and I take great joy in helping to raise Hannah.

Hannah's dad, however, is causing turmoil from afar. He has decided that he wants full custody and is on a mission to sabotage Hannah's relationship with her mom and me. My daughter allows him to bully her, and she is too intimidated to hire an attorney and file for divorce. As long as she does nothing legally, then Tom can get away with brainwashing Hannah and keeping our lives turned upside down.

Whenever Hannah returns from weekend visits with her dad, her demeanor changes and she becomes suspicious and distant toward me.

Besides the constant bad-mouthing, her dad also said that I hated him so much that I once tried to shoot him. Interesting, since I not only don't own a gun but have never touched one. He is trying to instill fear in her about me, so that she will want to live with him.

It takes me about three days to do damage control, and then we have two days of life back to normal before it's time to do it all over again. I can see the effects of the pressure that is put upon her; there is acting out at school and fearful behavior. This seems like a heavy burden to put upon a 7-year-old.

— *Pistol-Packing Grandma Kate*

Susan responds: This is a tough one because the most effective intervention is often a legal one. Bullies don't comply unless there are consequences such as jail, fines or losing what they have. Once a custody and visitation order is in place, not only are the parents required to follow it but there is also enforcement protection when they don't.

If, for instance, there is proof that one of the parents is practicing alienation tactics against the other parent to the child, then a clause most likely will be included in the order restraining such behavior. Sometimes judges find it necessary to demand the presence of a court-ordered monitor during visits. The judicial sector's foundation has been built on the protection of the child's best interests to include all phases of abuse, emotional or physical.

What's troubling is that emotional abuse is not visible, which makes it harder to track and therefore may not seem quite as real or serious as physical abuse. Brainwashing and parental or grandparent alienation are very real, destructive behaviors used by the abuser. This sets the child right in the middle of the adult conflict, where the child becomes torn and confused because suddenly they are being told who they can love.

A child's psyche is fragile during the developmental years, and close attention and concern is paramount from caregivers to the social services and legal systems. Emotional abuse is just as serious as physical abuse, and what's more, the scars sometimes never heal.

July - Aug 2011

Susan Hoffman is the author of Grand Wishes: Advocating to Preserve the Grandparent-Grandchild Bond and director of Advocates for Grandparent Grandchild Connection.

Chapter 11

EXAMPLES

This chapter is designed to give the reader a visual example of what is required in order to file a complete packet in court. The forms are specifically related to Orange County California, each state and county has their own. The use of photos, time line and persuasive declarations have no boundaries.

PHOTOS: Realistically 4 snapshots will fit on an 8 ½ by 11 paper:

2 Nov. '05

1 Oct. '05

4 Jan. '06

3 Dec. '05

DATE LOG OF VISITATION WITH JACOB : round 2

10-05-05: 3 hrs. eat, play, homework, tucked into bed.

10-07-05: 2 hrs. watched tv, talked.

10-12-05: 2 hrs. homework, asked me to sleepover.

10-22-05: Babysat 6 hrs. rode bikes, made lunch, drove Jacob alone to Target, helped clean rooms.

10-23-05: Visit at my house, Rubys for lunch, beach.

10-26-05: Phone visit

11-02-05: Phone visit

11-05-05: Babysat and stayed after 7 hrs. breakfast, lunch, cards, games.

11-09-05: Drove Jacob alone to Del Taco

11-16-05: phone visit

11-20-05: Drove Jacob to Thanksgiving party at other grandmas.

12-04-05: Drove Jacob alone out to dinner at Norms.

12-07-05: Phone visit

12-14-05: Attended Jacob's Xmas program

12-28-05:Gave Jacob, brother Xmas gifts

01-15-06: Attended Jacob's choir performance at church, later sat together and drew pictures.

06-18-06: 3 hrs. on the beach collecting shells with Jacob, Fathers Day.

WRITTEN DECLARATION, EXAMPLE 1:

I, Cindy Hill, Declare:

I am the biological grandmother of Rachel Brown, born February 25, 2009. I have actively participated in Rachel's life

since birth and starting when she was two weeks old, I was the sole caregiver while my daughter was at work and school. I have developed a bond with Rachel as she has with me, and believe a continuing relationship will be in her best interest. I am seeking a court order for contact and visitation with my granddaughter so we can continue our familial relationship.

During my babysitting time I noticed that when she arrived at my house she wasn't clean and clothing and bottles were often missing, so I picked up the slack and made sure that she was bathed, fed and well cared for, she began to thrive during my care. Our time together has resulted in a strong bond between us. My daughter is very young and I attributed the neglect to inexperience.

In September of 2009, I noticed some changes in my daughter, Autumn Taylor, Rachel's mother seemed forgetful, easily irritated and had mood swings. I was concerned with these signs because of her previous drug use, and when I confronted her she laughed. Autumn then became angry and verbally abusive, then stopped bringing Rachel to my home.

The inconsistent behavior continued, and when Rachel became sick, Autumn called upon me to care for the baby once again. I was more than willing to care for my granddaughter and do everything possible to nurse her back to health. When I noticed that the baby had arrived without food, proper medicine, or clean clothes, I once again discussed this with my daughter and she became irate. My son was involved this time, helping with transportation, and when he tried to communicate with his sister about her neglectful behavior toward the child, she blew up and threatened to never allow us to see Rachel again.

My greatest concern is for the well being of my granddaughter, and the stability, security and love that I am able to provide to her. I have made every effort to reestablish my relationship with my granddaughter, however Autumn refuses to let me visit or interact with Rachel. I believe it is important to Rachel's welfare to maintain a loving relationship with me, her maternal grandmother.

WRITTEN DECLARATION, example 2:

Vera Crawford: declaration outline

I am the biological grandmother of Dean Kenney, born Feb. 12, 2004; I was there that day and it was the best day of my life.

Katherine Martin and my son, Nicholas Kenney lived together but were never married. The first time that they separated was when Dean was 3 months old.

Even though the parents were not getting along, I managed to maintain my relationship with Katherine and Dean, soon they began to rely on me both financially and emotionally, which was fine with me because I enjoyed spending time with my grandson more than anything. We soon developed a strong BOND as I babysat 3 days per week during my days off with at least 1 weekly overnight. I took turns spending time with Dean going back and forth between each parent's residence. This put me in a difficult position, but I wanted to help both parents and remain a stable force in his life.

My son and his girlfriend had a volatile relationship and as things escalated between them, Katherine began to distance herself from me and along with that my grandparenting time was reduced.

When Dean was about 2 years old, my son got into some trouble with alcohol and ended up doing some jail time. My son chose rehabilitation and because I supported him, Katherine ultimately refused me visitation with my grandson. For 3 years my son fought in court to regain his visitation and custody rights and for 3 years I accompanied him to weekly monitored visits with Dean. We made the most out of the time the 3 of us had together, enjoying lots of one on one quiet time, play time and taking Nolan on many family oriented excursions.

When Dean was 4 years old, his dad, my son passed away from an accidental drug overdose. My grief is beyond explanation, but little Dean has not only lost his father but now his grandmother and all ties to his paternal family.

I have sent cards, gifts, emails, made telephone calls yet I have still not seen Dean since just before his father died Sept. 20, 2008. Katherine has avoided me or made excuses whenever I try to make arrangements for a visit. The closest I have been allowed into his life is when she sends MYSPACE photos of him.

I believe that I continue to be punished for my son's actions and his estranged relationship with Katherine. I want to maintain the BOND that I have with Dean and continue our relationship with consistent visits. I dearly love Dean and I believe it is in his best interest to be a part of his father's family and maintain a connection to his heritage.

Sample Request for Grandparent Visitation Form:

ATTORNEY *(Name & Address)*:	FOR COURT USE ONLY
TELEPHONE NO.: FAX NO. (Optional): E-MAIL ADDRESS (Optional): ATTORNEY FOR *(Name)*: BAR NO.:	
SUPERIOR COURT OF CALIFORNIA, COUNTY OF ORANGE JUSTICE CENTER: ☐ Lamoreaux – 341 The City Drive, Orange, CA 92868-3205 ☐ Central – 700 Civic Center Drive West, Santa Ana, CA 92701	
PETITIONER: RESPONDENT:	
PETITION FOR GRANDPARENT VISITATION	CASE NUMBER:

1. Petitioner's relationship to minor child(ren) listed below:

   ☐ grandmother   ☐ grandfather

   ☐ my son *(name)* _____ is the parent of the child(ren).

   ☐ my daughter *(name)* _____ is the parent of the child(ren).

Child's name	Birthdate	Currently living with *(relationship)* / in *(county)*	Other Parent's Name
_____	_____	_____	_____
_____	_____	_____	_____
_____	_____	_____	_____
_____	_____	_____	_____
_____	_____	_____	_____

2. The parents of the child(ren) *(mark all boxes and complete all spaces which apply)*:

   a. ☐ are currently married or have a domestic partnership and living together.

   b. ☐ are divorced. A Judgment for Dissolution of Marriage or Domestic Partnership was entered on:

   (specify date) _____, in _____ County, *(state)* _____

   Case No. _____.

   c. ☐ are currently involved in a divorce proceeding in _____ County, Case No. _____.

   d. ☐ are currently married or have a domestic partnership and one of the parents has been absent for more than one month without the other parent knowing the whereabouts of the absent parent.

   e. ☐ have never been married or in a domestic partnership.

   f. ☐ are currently living separate and apart on a permanent or indefinite basis.

   g. ☐ The ☐ mother ☐ father   of the minor child(ren) is deceased.

   h. ☐ The child(ren) is/are not residing with either parent.

   i. ☐ The child(ren) has/have been adopted by a ☐ stepparent ☐ grandparent ☐other *(specify relationship and name)*: _____.

Approved for Optional Use
L-0373 [New September 14, 2009] **PETITION FOR GRANDPARENT VISITATION** Family Code §§ 3102, 3103, 3104
Cal. Rules of Court 5.150, 5.154(b), 5.156, 5.158

Sample Summons Form:

SUM-100

SUMMONS
(CITACION JUDICIAL)

NOTICE TO DEFENDANT:
(AVISO AL DEMANDADO):

YOU ARE BEING SUED BY PLAINTIFF:
(LO ESTÁ DEMANDANDO EL DEMANDANTE):

To keep other people from seeing what you entered on your form, please press the Clear This Form button at the end of the form when finished.

NOTICE! You have been sued. The court may decide against you without your being heard unless you respond within 30 days. Read the information below.

You have 30 CALENDAR DAYS after this summons and legal papers are served on you to file a written response at this court and have a copy served on the plaintiff. A letter or phone call will not protect you. Your written response must be in proper legal form if you want the court to hear your case. There may be a court form that you can use for your response. You can find these court forms and more information at the California Courts Online Self-Help Center (*www.courtinfo.ca.gov/selfhelp*), your county law library, or the courthouse nearest you. If you cannot pay the filing fee, ask the court clerk for a fee waiver form. If you do not file your response on time, you may lose the case by default, and your wages, money, and property may be taken without further warning from the court.

There are other legal requirements. You may want to call an attorney right away. If you do not know an attorney, you may want to call an attorney referral service. If you cannot afford an attorney, you may be eligible for free legal services from a nonprofit legal services program. You can locate these nonprofit groups at the California Legal Services Web site (*www.lawhelpcalifornia.org*), the California Courts Online Self-Help Center (*www.courtinfo.ca.gov/selfhelp*), or by contacting your local court or county bar association. **NOTE:** The court has a statutory lien for waived fees and costs on any settlement or arbitration award of $10,000 or more in a civil case. The court's lien must be paid before the court will dismiss the case.

¡AVISO! Lo han demandado. Si no responde dentro de 30 días, la corte puede decidir en su contra sin escuchar su versión. Lea la información a continuación.

Tiene 30 DÍAS DE CALENDARIO después de que le entreguen esta citación y papeles legales para presentar una respuesta por escrito en esta corte y hacer que se entregue una copia al demandante. Una carta o una llamada telefónica no lo protegen. Su respuesta por escrito tiene que estar en formato legal correcto si desea que procesen su caso en la corte. Es posible que haya un formulario que usted pueda usar para su respuesta. Puede encontrar estos formularios de la corte y más información en el Centro de Ayuda de las Cortes de California (www.sucorte.ca.gov), en la biblioteca de leyes de su condado o en la corte que le quede más cerca. Si no puede pagar la cuota de presentación, pida al secretario de la corte que le dé un formulario de exención de pago de cuotas. Si no presenta su respuesta a tiempo, puede perder el caso por incumplimiento y la corte le podrá quitar su sueldo, dinero y bienes sin más advertencia.

Hay otros requisitos legales. Es recomendable que llame a un abogado inmediatamente. Si no conoce a un abogado, puede llamar a un servicio de remisión a abogados. Si no puede pagar a un abogado, es posible que cumpla con los requisitos para obtener servicios legales gratuitos de un programa de servicios legales sin fines de lucro. Puede encontrar estos grupos sin fines de lucro en el sitio web de California Legal Services, (www.lawhelpcalifornia.org), en el Centro de Ayuda de las Cortes de California, (www.sucorte.ca.gov) o poniéndose en contacto con la corte o el colegio de abogados locales. AVISO: Por ley, la corte tiene derecho a reclamar las cuotas y los costos exentos por imponer un gravamen sobre cualquier recuperación de $10,000 ó más de valor recibida mediante un acuerdo o una concesión de arbitraje en un caso de derecho civil. Tiene que pagar el gravamen de la corte antes de que la corte pueda desechar el caso.

The name and address of the court is: *(El nombre y dirección de la corte es):*	CASE NUMBER: *(Número del Caso):*

The name, address, and telephone number of plaintiff's attorney, or plaintiff without an attorney, is:
(El nombre, la dirección y el número de teléfono del abogado del demandante, o del demandante que no tiene abogado, es):

DATE: *(Fecha)*	Clerk, by *(Secretario)*	, Deputy *(Adjunto)*

(For proof of service of this summons, use Proof of Service of Summons (form POS-010).)
(Para prueba de entrega de esta citatión use el formulario Proof of Service of Summons, (POS-010)).

[SEAL]

NOTICE TO THE PERSON SERVED: You are served
1. ☐ as an individual defendant.
2. ☐ as the person sued under the fictitious name of *(specify):*

3. ☐ on behalf of *(specify):*

  under: ☐ CCP 416.10 (corporation)   ☐ CCP 416.60 (minor)
  ☐ CCP 416.20 (defunct corporation)   ☐ CCP 416.70 (conservatee)
  ☐ CCP 416.40 (association or partnership) ☐ CCP 416.90 (authorized person)
  ☐ other *(specify):*
4. ☐ by personal delivery on *(date):*

Page 1 of 1

Form Adopted for Mandatory Use
Judicial Council of California
SUM-100 [Rev. July 1, 2009]

SUMMONS

Code of Civil Procedure §§ 412.20, 465
www.courtinfo.ca.gov

Save This Form | **Print This Form** | **Clear This Form** | For your protection and privacy, please press the Clear This Form button after you

Sample Declaration Form:

FL-105/GC-120

ATTORNEY OR PARTY WITHOUT ATTORNEY *(Name, State Bar number, and address):*

TELEPHONE NO.:
FAX NO. *(Optional):*
E-MAIL ADDRESS *(Optional):*
ATTORNEY FOR *(Name):*

SUPERIOR COURT OF CALIFORNIA, COUNTY OF

STREET ADDRESS:
MAILING ADDRESS:
CITY AND ZIP CODE:
BRANCH NAME:

PETITIONER: *(This section applies only to family law cases.)*
RESPONDENT:
OTHER PARTY:

(This section applies only to guardianship cases.)
GUARDIANSHIP OF *(Name):*   Minor

CASE NUMBER:

**DECLARATION UNDER UNIFORM CHILD CUSTODY
JURISDICTION AND ENFORCEMENT ACT (UCCJEA)**

1. **I am a party** to this proceeding to determine custody of a child.

2. ☐ My present address and the present address of each child residing with me is confidential under Family Code section 3429 as I have indicated in item 3.

3. There are *(specify number):*   minor children who are subject to this proceeding, as follows:
   (Insert the information requested below. The residence information must be given for the last FIVE years.)

a. Child's name		Place of birth	Date of birth	Sex
Period of residence	Address	Person child lived with *(name and complete current address)*		Relationship
to present	☐ Confidential	☐ Confidential		
to	Child's residence *(City, State)*	Person child lived with *(name and complete current address)*		
to	Child's residence *(City, State)*	Person child lived with *(name and complete current address)*		
to	Child's residence *(City, State)*	Person child lived with *(name and complete current address)*		
b. Child's name		Place of birth	Date of birth	Sex
☐ Residence information is the same as given above for child a. *(If NOT the same, provide the information below.)*				
Period of residence	Address	Person child lived with *(name and complete current address)*		Relationship
to present	☐ Confidential	☐ Confidential		
to	Child's residence *(City, State)*	Person child lived with *(name and complete current address)*		
to	Child's residence *(City, State)*	Person child lived with *(name and complete current address)*		
to	Child's residence *(City, State)*	Person child lived with *(name and complete current address)*		

c. ☐ Additional residence information for a child listed in item a or b is continued on attachment 3c.

d. ☐ Additional children are listed on form FL-105(A)/GC-120(A). *(Provide all requested information for additional children.)*

Page 1 of 2

Form Adopted for Mandatory Use
Judicial Council of California
FL-105/GC-120 [Rev. January 1, 2009]

**DECLARATION UNDER UNIFORM CHILD CUSTODY
JURISDICTION AND ENFORCEMENT ACT (UCCJEA)**

Family Code, § 3400 et seq.,
Probate Code, §§ 1510(f), 1512
www.courtinfo.ca.gov

Sample Order to Show Cause Form:

FL-300

ATTORNEY OR PARTY WITHOUT ATTORNEY *(Name, State Bar number, and address):*	To keep other people from seeing what you entered on your form, please press the Clear This Form button at the end of the form when

TELEPHONE NO.: FAX NO. *(Optional):*
E-MAIL ADDRESS *(Optional):*
ATTORNEY FOR *(Name):*

SUPERIOR COURT OF CALIFORNIA, COUNTY OF

STREET ADDRESS:
MAILING ADDRESS:
CITY AND ZIP CODE:
BRANCH NAME:

PETITIONER/PLAINTIFF:
RESPONDENT/DEFENDANT:

ORDER TO SHOW CAUSE	**MODIFICATION**		CASE NUMBER:
☐ Child Custody	☐ Visitation	☐ Injunctive Order	
☐ Child Support	☐ Spousal Support	☐ Other *(specify):*	
☐ Attorney Fees and Costs			

1. TO *(name):*
2. YOU ARE ORDERED TO APPEAR IN THIS COURT AS FOLLOWS TO GIVE ANY LEGAL REASON WHY THE RELIEF SOUGHT IN THE ATTACHED APPLICATION SHOULD NOT BE GRANTED. **If child custody or visitation is an issue in this proceeding, Family Code section 3170 requires mediation before or concurrently with the hearing listed below.**

   a. Date: Time: ☐ Dept.:   ☐ Room:

   b. The address of the court is ☐ same as noted above ☐ other *(specify):*

   c. ☐ The parties are ordered to attend custody mediation services as follows:

3. THE COURT FURTHER ORDERS that a completed *Application for Order and Supporting Declaration* (form FL-310), a **blank** *Responsive Declaration* (form FL-320), and the following documents be served with this order:

   a. (1) ☐ Completed *Income and Expense Declaration* (form FL-150) and a **blank** *Income and Expense Declaration*
      (2) ☐ Completed *Financial Statement (Simplified)* (form FL-155) and a **blank** *Financial Statement (Simplified)*
      (3) ☐ Completed *Property Declaration* (form FL-160) and a **blank** *Property Declaration*
      (4) ☐ Points and authorities
      (5) ☐ Other *(specify):*

   b. ☐ Time for ☐ service ☐ hearing is shortened. Service must be on or before *(date):*
      Any responsive declaration must be served on or before *(date):*
   c. ☐ You are ordered to comply with the temporary orders attached.
   d. ☐ Other *(specify):*

Date: _____

                  JUDICIAL OFFICER

NOTICE: If you have children from this relationship, the court is required to order payment of child support based on the incomes of both parents. The amount of child support can be large. It normally continues until the child is 18. You should supply the court with information about your finances. Otherwise, the child support order will be based on the information supplied by the other parent.

You do not have to pay any fee to file declarations in response to this order to show cause (including a completed Income and Expense Declaration (form FL-150) or Financial Statement *(Simplified)* (form FL-155) that will show your finances). In the absence of an order shortening time, the original of the responsive declaration must be filed with the court and a copy served on the other party at least nine court days before the hearing date. Add five calendar days if you serve by mail within California. (See Code of Civil Procedure 1005 for other situations.) To determine court and calendar days, go to *www.courtinfo.ca.gov/selfhelp/courtcalendars/.*

Requests for Accommodations
Assistive listening systems, computer-assisted real-time captioning, or sign language interpreter services are available if you ask at least five days before the proceeding. Contact the clerk's office or go to *www.courtinfo.ca.gov/forms* for *Request for Accommodations by Persons With Disabilities and Response* (Form MC-410). (Civil Code, § 54.8.)

Page 1 of 1

Form Adopted for Mandatory Use Judicial Council of California FL-300 [Rev. January 1, 2007]	**ORDER TO SHOW CAUSE**	Family Code, §§ 215, 270 et seq., 3000 et seq., 3500 et seq., 4300 www.courtinfo.ca.gov

For your protection and privacy, please press the Clear This Form button after you   Save This Form   Print This Form   Clear This Form

Sample Order & Supporting Declaration Form:

FL-310

PETITIONER/PLAINTIFF:	CASE NUMBER:
RESPONDENT/DEFENDANT:	

APPLICATION FOR ORDER AND SUPPORTING DECLARATION
—THIS IS NOT AN ORDER—

☐ Petitioner ☐ Respondent ☐ Claimant requests the following orders:

1. ☐ CHILD CUSTODY ☐ To be ordered pending the hearing
   a. Child's name and age
   b. Legal custody to (name of person who makes decisions about health, education, etc.)
   c. Physical custody to (name of person with whom child will live.)

   d. ☐ Modify existing order
      (1) filed on (date):
      (2) ordering (specify):
   e. ☐ As requested in form ☐ FL-311 ☐ FL-312 ☐ FL-341(C) ☐ FL-341(D) ☐ FL-341(E)

2. ☐ CHILD VISITATION ☐ To be ordered pending the hearing
   a. As requested in: (1) ☐ Attachment 2a (2) ☐ Form FL-311 (3) ☐ Other (specify):
   b. ☐ Modify existing order
      (1) filed on (date):
      (2) ordering (specify):
   c. ☐ One or more domestic violence restraining/protective orders are now in effect. (Attach a copy of the orders if you have one.) The orders are from the following court or courts (specify county and state):
      (1) ☐ Criminal: County/state: (3) ☐ Juvenile: County/state:
          Case No. (if known):   Case No. (if known):
      (2) ☐ Family: County/state: (4) ☐ Other: County/state:
          Case No. (if known):   Case No. (if known):

3. ☐ CHILD SUPPORT (An earnings assignment order may be issued.)
   a. Child's name and age
   b. Monthly amount requested (if not by guideline)
      $

   c. ☐ Modify existing order
      (1) filed on (date):
      (2) ordering (specify):

4. ☐ SPOUSAL OR PARTNER SUPPORT (An earnings assignment order may be issued.)
   a. ☐ Amount requested (monthly): $ c. ☐ Modify existing order
   b. ☐ Terminate existing order   (1) filed on (date):
      (1) filed on (date):   (2) ordering (specify):
      (2) ordering (specify):

NOTE: To obtain domestic violence restraining orders, you must use the forms *Request for Order (Domestic Violence Prevention)* (form DV-100), *Temporary Restraining Order (Domestic Violence Prevention)* (form DV-110), and *Notice of Court Hearing (Domestic Violence Prevention)* (form DV-109).

Page 1 of 2

Form Adopted for Mandatory Use Judicial Council of California FL-310 [Rev. July 1, 2011]	**APPLICATION FOR ORDER AND SUPPORTING DECLARATION**	Family Code, §§ 2045, 2107, 6224, 8226, 6320–6326, 6380–6383 www.courtinfo.ca.gov

Sample Custody/Visitation Form:

FL-311

| PETITIONER/PLAINTIFF: | CASE NUMBER: |
| RESPONDENT/DEFENDANT: | |

CHILD CUSTODY AND VISITATION APPLICATION ATTACHMENT

TO ☐ Petition, Response, Application for Order or Responsive Declaration ☐ Other *(specify):*

☐ To be ordered now and effective until the hearing

1. ☐ **Custody.** Custody of the minor children of the parties is requested as follows:

| Child's Name | Date of Birth | Legal Custody to *(person who makes decisions about health, education, etc.)* | Physical Custody to *(person with whom the child lives)* |

2. ☐ **Visitation.**

a. ☐ Reasonable right of visitation to the party without physical custody (**not appropriate in cases involving domestic violence**)

b. ☐ See the attached _____-page document dated *(specify date):*

c. ☐ The parties will go to mediation at *(specify location):*

d. ☐ No visitation

e. ☐ Visitation for the ☐ petitioner ☐ respondent will be as follows:

(1) ☐ **Weekends starting** *(date):*

(The first weekend of the month is the first weekend with a Saturday.)

☐ 1st ☐ 2nd ☐ 3rd ☐ 4th ☐ 5th weekend of the month

from _____ at _____ ☐ a.m. ☐ p.m.
    (day of week)   *(time)*

to _____ at _____ ☐ a.m. ☐ p.m.
   (day of week)   *(time)*

(a) ☐ The parents will alternate the fifth weekends, with the ☐ petitioner ☐ respondent having the initial fifth weekend, which starts *(date):*

(b) ☐ The petitioner will have fifth weekends in ☐ odd ☐ even months.

(2) ☐ **Alternate weekends starting** *(date):*

The ☐ petitioner ☐ respondent will have the children with him or her during the period

from _____ at _____ ☐ a.m. ☐ p.m.
    (day of week)   *(time)*

to _____ at _____ ☐ a.m. ☐ p.m.
   (day of week)   *(time)*

(3) ☐ **Weekdays starting** *(date):*

The ☐ petitioner ☐ respondent will have the children with him or her during the period

from _____ at _____ ☐ a.m. ☐ p.m.
    (day of week)   *(time)*

to _____ at _____ ☐ a.m. ☐ p.m.
   (day of week)   *(time)*

(4) ☐ **Other** *(specify days and times as well as any additional restrictions):*

☐ See Attachment 2e(4).

Page 1 of 2

Form Approved for Optional Use
Judicial Council of California
FL-311 [Rev. July 1, 2005]

CHILD CUSTODY AND VISITATION APPLICATION ATTACHMENT

Family Code, § 6200 et seq.
www.courtinfo.ca.gov

Sample Notice Related Case Form:

<table>
<tr>
<td>ATTORNEY OR PARTY WITHOUT ATTORNEY (Name & Address):</td>
<td>FOR COURT USE ONLY</td>
</tr>
<tr>
<td>

TELEPHONE NO.:   FAX NO. (Optional):
E-MAIL ADDRESS (Optional):
ATTORNEY FOR (Name):   BAR NO.:
</td>
<td></td>
</tr>
</table>

SUPERIOR COURT OF CALIFORNIA, COUNTY OF ORANGE
JUSTICE CENTER:
☐ Central - 700 Civic Center Dr. West, Santa Ana, CA 92701-4045
☐ Lamoreaux - 341 The City Drive, Orange, CA 92868-3205

PLAINTIFF/PETITIONER:

DEFENDANT/RESPONDENT:

FAMILY LAW NOTICE RE RELATED CASE	CASE NUMBER:

The parties must file this form with the Superior Court of Orange County, when a family law case is filed with the Court and when a party discovers that there is a related case. **A related case means one or both parties and/or minor children of the parties are involved in other cases.** Examples of related cases include another family law case, a domestic violence case, a child support collection case, a criminal case, and a juvenile case involving a minor child of one or both of the parties.

Fill in the requested information:

1.   I also used the name(s): _____
_____

2.   The other party's name is: _____;
He/She has also used the name(s): _____
_____

3.   ☐ Other court cases involving either party or a child of either party:
(If known, please include the case numbers)

	Case Number	Case Name	Court Location/ Justice Center	Person Involved
a.				
b.				
c.				
d.				

4.   ☐ There are no other court cases involving either party or a child of either party.

Date:

_____   _____
(TYPE OR PRINT NAME OF PARTY OR ATTORNEY)   (SIGNATURE OF PARTY OR ATTORNEY)

Page 1 of 1

Approved for Optional Use
Form # L-1120
Rev. May 5, 2010

FAMILY LAW NOTICE RE RELATED CASE

Superior Court of Orange County
Local Rule 701.5
www.occourts.org

• The State Legislature decides what the fees are to file different kinds of family law forms. As of this date 2011, California filing fees are $395.00.

• Fee waivers are also available to those who qualify.

• Superior Courts retain a self help center and online forms are available for downloading and printing.

• Forms differ according to situation, consulting an attorney advisable.

Chapter 12

GRANDPARENT FEEDBACK

1. A Grandma without contact:

Quick catch up regarding the girls. I follow along with their school events via a newsletter. Family is still tight lipped and refuse to share a bone with us. I just try to keep up with my website and journal to them monthly. Per your gentle book, I never write or say a word that is negative regarding my son or their mother. I know it would only fuel an already blazing fire.

And so, we sit and wait and hope and pray we all will someday get a break. If you ever get a minute watch the movie *In Her Shoes*.

It is not exactly our situation, but it certainly shows how grandchildren can be told a whole lot of nonsense.

The public and the court system needs to know, and give a care as to the long term effects of what grandparent dismissal will have on our beloved grandchildren.

I keep saying over and over the children have no voice, they have no choice. In our justice system, we are taught that one is innocent until proven guilty.

Not so with grandparents. We are denied, tossed aside and exiled without due cause with no trial, with no explanation needed by the system, and society sits in wonder why our children are so dysfunctional, on anti depressants by the age of 12.

I could go on, but all we need to do is read the Internet or pick up a newspaper.

It seems that everything today is disposable, including grandparents, who were once the voice of reason, unconditional love, respected, and wise.

Take Care, Thank you for your tireless efforts

and I think about you often."

xo, Nikki

2. A Grandpa marching on fragile territory:

Susan, your website is very impressive, but your experience made me feel so sad and that my situation is really minor compared to yours. Sadly, the courts don't give value to what grandparents unconditional love adds to a child's life-often giving them the warmth they don't get from either parent. Judges need to be educated, as well as the psycs who make the reports and rarely, if ever comment on the grandparents' role.

Ron

3. Grandparents with limited access:

I want to share a little of what I have gone through in order to visit with my 3 year old grandson. Today was the first time we saw him since August when we had to leave him with strangers at the CPS office in Murrieta.

We went before the judge yesterday and the parents fought hard not wanting to let me have visitation, they kept saying we do not have rights.

I asked for supervised visitation because I wanted documentation sent back to the courts after the visits.

My husband and I saw Ethan today and when it was time to leave his face spoke a million words. He kept looking back at us and I assured him that we would see him again.

His eyes showed sadness. We believe this is only the beginning though.

Best Regards, and bless you for all that you do,

Joanna

4. A Grandma with court ordered visits:

Michele said our visits are her favorite thing to do. She still looks at me as if she wants to know why we don't see her like we used to, as if she'd done something wrong, and she hasn't seen her bedroom in our home in 2 years. Without your efforts I'd probably still be on the floor in Michele's room in the fetal position crying my heart out. The question is "how do we make others feel the child's pain"? Why do we have to wait for each grandparent to feel the way we do in order for it to happen? I think you're doing a great job and plowing through.

Carol

5. A Grandma without contact:

I don't think people realize that there are many grand-parents in our same situation. It is something that isn't spoken about so the public doesn't realize it is happening all over the US. I guess all we can do is educate the public more until people realize it is something that should be recognized.

Jean

6. A Grandma with visits:

I really do want to come to a meeting soon. I was so fortunate that the path I took to be able to be in Tony's life ended up the way it did. I get him basically whenever I want to these days and many times he asks his dad before I do if he can come for a weekend. When he's at my house he always tells me how much he loves to come over - I think it reminds him of his mom. He still misses her terribly. He has numerous behavioral problems that go along with the environment he is being raised in with his dad and the many other druggies he's around but I am so grateful for the outcome of getting to see him. I think our generation tends to want to control our kids on into adulthood and as much as I dislike Gary and how Tony is being raised, I had to come to grips with the reality that he is Tony's dad and let that one go. I honor what was and is requested of me and it works.

I ache for all of those that are still denied access.... grandparents are the special unconditional love givers in grandchildren's lives.

If we can learn to give our children that same kind of love I think it opens up the possibility to bridge the gap. Every child, no matter how young or old, wants to know their parents love and accept them for who they are...

I look forward to seeing you soon.

Jill

7. Grandparents with court ordered visits:

The visit was wonderful. Hayley spotted us up the hill as soon as her game ended (we got to see her play a bit). She ran to the fence and was calling us. She came out and hugged us and told us how she was counting the days.

We decorated cookies for Hayley to take home, she made her mom a birthday card, and we played all day. She so enjoys all the attention of us doing what she wants. I told her that her mommy was concerned about not having a place for the pumpkin, but if she still wanted to carve it, I'd love to have it at my house so I can show all the neighbors. She liked that idea and carved both pumpkins. She mentioned something she'd wanted and I told her Christmas was coming...she said, "It's always like Christmas when I'm with you grammy."

Betty & Greg

8. Standing up for a child:

Happy Mother's Day Grandma, I love you!

I replay those words every day from a recordable card that my granddaughter sent me for Mother's Day in 2009.

I listen to her words, her sweet little voice, as a daily reminder of why I have been fighting for her rights since the beginning of 2008. I know in my heart that if she understood what has been happening to our family, she would do anything she could to stay in our lives.

Mine is a long story, as are most of these stories, but for now, for today, for this blog, I will keep it simple. My granddaughter came into our family in 2005 and as I cut the umbilical cord, our bond began. For numerous reasons, two years ago, we were slowly cut out of her life. It's been an excruciatingly painful journey and with much effort and support, we are in the process of reuniting, but not without legal support. AFGGC has played a huge role in how I got my foot in the courtroom door and I am forever grateful for that, and for Susan Hoffman...

The bottom line here is seek all outlets of support, trust your gut, be tough enough to withstand the journey, and most importantly, never, ever, ever give up!

Kathy

9. Be There

I now understand after reading your book and being a part of the educational process that the most important role a grandparent can have is to be there for the family. I cannot change the way they live because I am not in charge. We grandparents must learn to accept the lifestyle that the parents have chosen for themselves and for their children, whether we like it or not.

It doesn't matter if they live in a one room shack or have conflicting values and religious beliefs from mine, there is nothing I can do about it.

What matters is that I love them and will be there for all of them. So, I keep my mouth shut and make myself ready, willing and able to be there.

Grandpa Mark

Chapter 13

Life Isn't Fair: Is It Supposed To Be?

We live in a world where animals have more rights than children. In the United States, parents are required to feed, clothe and provide shelter to a child, that's it. They are also not allowed to neglect or physically abuse their children, however that must be proven.

Once again I will ask the question, how does someone take a loving grandparent from a child after they have established a bond? Does anyone care about emotional abuse? Emotional abuse takes a backseat to physical abuse even though this seems like this is a rather abusive way of treating a child. Parent's who disregard a child's best interests, clearly are not putting the child's needs first. The parents are not thinking about the child's feelings, it simply does not matter that an attachment has been broken by "unreasonably denying" the grandparent. To clarify, "unreasonably denied" meaning there is no good reason to deny and therefore break that attachment that a child has formed with a grandparent unless the grandparent is a danger. Family feuds may be a reason to make changes in circumstances for visitation, but never to cut off the child from a grandparent. They have a whole and separate relationship with the grandparent so realistically what goes on between the parent and grand-parent should not be affected. But it is, so the unreasonable then becomes the reason; all parents have a reason. Knowing that unreasonable to some is a reason to the ones who control the access, it's best to operate on the assumption that parent's don't really need an approved reason to deny access to a child.

Grandparents must be on their best behavior at all times. What they think does not matter when it comes to maintaining visitation. In order to get along with the "me" generation of parents, grandparents may well want to shift into that program. Go along so you can get along.

Things are different now, nothing is like the way things were when we boomers were growing up. Back then we respected our Grands. We depended on them and so did our parents. We were all part of an extended family. Today grandparents are still caregivers when parents are no longer fit to raise their children, and also when economical factors drive families back together. Geography and technology has been the driving force in the development of nuclear based family lifestyle.

Another example of bringing unnecessary suffering upon a child is the dissolution of family when one of the parents dies. It is not uncommon these days for the surviving parent to cut off the parents of the parent who died. As sick as that sounds, it happens a lot.

The child grieves the loss of a parent and the parent of that parent, the grandparent, grieves the loss of losing a child. To top it off they lose whatever they have left, each other. Nope life truly is not fair, even in the land of optimism. Children do not have Liberty Interests: said differently: No voice no choice all the more reason that grandparents must do whatever it takes to stay close. *"A Precious Bond,"* should not be broken.

For Information About Grandparent Visitation Issues:

ADVOCATES FOR GRANDPARENT GRANDCHILD CONNECTION, 501 © (3)

www.grandparentchildconnect.org

PO BOX 5622

Newport Beach, Cal. 92662

949-640-0399

AFGGC@grandwishes.org